Quilting
the Savory Garden

SANDRA MILLETT

An F&W Publications Company

700 East State Street • Iola, WI 54990-0001
715-445-2214 • 888-457-2873
www.krause.com

Published by

Please call or write for our free catalog of publications. To place an order or obtain a free catalog, please call 800-258-0929. Please use our regular business telephone, 715-445-2214, for editorial comment or further information.

Library of Congress Catalog Number 2003101333
ISBN 0-87349-559-4

Acknowledgments

Words seem such feeble testimony to thank those who made this book possible. Generous corporate support from Pfaff, Koala Cabinets, YLI Corporation, Clover Needlecraft, Inc., Creative Grids, and Electric Quilt Company made my job easier. Jan Carr and Rob Krieger deserve extra kudos.

It has been a pleasure working with Krause Publications, through both Julie Stephani, and Christine Townsend, my editor.

Quilting and writing friends kept me focused and supplied laughs when my days became too long or the computer too threatening. My gratitude especially goes to my dear friend, Becky Harness, of Old Town Quilts. A special thanks goes to the Trinity Writers Workshop of Bedford, Texas; reading portions of this text was above and beyond, especially for the men. During one critique, I found out that they thought a sewer refers to plumbing problems.

And for my husband, there are not enough kind words. He gave up vacations with only mild grumbling, became an expert at handling the camera while I had both hands occupied in front of the lens with needle and fabric, and endured a messy house with grace.

Contents

Introduction

What a Garden! *fabrics were selected with a" let-her-rip" attitude in color and fabric patterns. This is my favorite of the two quilts.*

The Savory Garden *quilt using traditional colors. Machine quilted by Becky Harness.*

GETTING STARTED

Welcome to my Savory Garden. I hope you enjoy creating your own quilt as much as I liked designing and making the samples. Whether you are a beginner or an experienced quilter, these patterns were developed with you in mind. Every chapter incorporates new techniques, challenges, and options along with concise, step-by-step instructions.

Do not be daunted by a block's technical appearance. When a new technique is introduced, detailed instructions with line art or photographs demonstrate the finer points. However, these instructions are given only once; thereafter, you are referred back to the block where the technique was introduced.

Whether you choose real-life or nontraditional colors, machine or handwork for the appliqué and piecing, or a combination of both, I stress *accuracy*. When finished, your quilt should be square, lay flat, and not be ruffled on the edges. To achieve blocks that are true-to-size, three things are essential: Accuracy in marking, cutting, and piecing. At no time will I tell you to "true-up" a

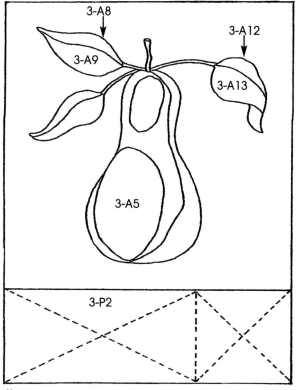

Illus. I-1

All patterns are keyed to a chapter and the letter refers to technique: Appliqué (A), or Piecing (P). The number after the dash indicates the specific patch and/or the sewing order.

block, except where heavy machine embellishing may shrink the fabric. Resizing assumes from the start that the block is inaccurate. I approach quiltmaking from the opposite direction—that your quilt *is* accurate. This book tells you how to make it that way.

PATTERN NUMBERING

All blocks are keyed and numbered in the same manner, and the blocks are listed in order of teaching techniques. Chapter 3, The Pear (see Illus. 1-1, below), is pieced and appliquéd. Appliqué shapes are labeled with an "A," pieced patches with "P." The first number refers to the block, while the letter and the number following the hyphen refer to technique and its specific patch. Therefore, 3-A12 is the top appliqué patch of the leaf on the right in Chapter 3, and 3-P2 is the largest pieced triangle. Appliqué patches are sewn in numbering sequence.

DECIDE ON A LIGHT SOURCE BEFORE SELECTING FABRICS

What do all paintings have in common? Each one has a single light source, so that shadows fall in the same direction. To paint with fabric, your quilt must also have a single light source. Just answer one question: From what direction is the light shining? Is it from the upper left corner, or the upper right corner? Once the decision has been made, choose fabrics and make color placement decisions just as artists who apply oil paint on canvas do. Being consistent with the light source throughout the same quilt creates a cohesive, believable look.

In my **Savory Garden** quilt made with real-life colors, the light source is from the upper left. Leaves are lighter, and highlights brighter that face toward, or are closer to, the upper left of every block. In the **What a Garden!** quilt made with vibrant, non-traditional colors, the light source comes from the upper right.

At times, the colors may be subtle, but in some areas there is no doubt about the direction of the light. Study the pear blocks in each quilt. Here again, the choice is yours: Strong contrast, understated contrast, or a combination of the two convey a specific mood.

Study the top left leaf of the traditional pear

Side-by-side comparisons of the pear block in Chapter 2. Notice how the fabrics reflect the light source that comes from the high left on the left pear, and the high right on the nontraditional block.

The leaf's top is positioned to take advantage of the lightest portion of the print. The bottom segment takes advantage of a dark streak to simulate the vein.

block. 3-A8 was positioned so that the lightest part of the fabric is at its center; the shaded side farthest away from the sun is darker. The right leaf has the light side on the bottom, even though logic says that side is shaded. I wanted to make 3-A13 puff up, as if that section of the leaf curved toward the sun. The top is darker and drops back, while the most shadowed underside of the leaf receives the least light.

Now compare the fabric choices in **What a Garden!** pear, above. The right leaf is the closest to the sun so the top gets the most light, while the lower portion is darker and the underside is darker still since it is in full shadow.

THE IMPORTANCE OF FABRIC PATTERN

Fabric design, along with colors and the light source, contributes to making a flat shape appear three-dimensional. Fabric design adds depth and interest that creates movement and life. Selecting portions of a fabric's design to enhance a highlight, shadow, or curve intensify the final effect. Cutting fabrics with these criteria in mind is called "fussy-cutting." Fussy-cutting certainly turns your yardage into an imitation of Swiss cheese. In **What A Garden!**, the selection of light yellow in the pear's 3-A8 upper leaf is no accident. The fabric design is deliberately placed so that the bright yellow is at the tip, and the darker colors are closer to the stem. Then 3-A9 is positioned to utilize a dark streak that enhances the center vein, stresses the leaf's shape, and creates a more three-dimensional appearance.

Study the photo of the pear's body, below. The light source is high on the right, so the right side of the pear is highlighted. When I appliquéd the plaid highlight to the pattern's edge, however, the lighter fabric color blended into the background fabric and visually disappeared. To solve this problem, the checkered patch was removed and shifted left, leaving a 1/16" strip of the darker pear body showing on the right edge.

Creating a darker outline against a light background is a visual trick that painters have used for centuries, but the technique has not been seen in appliqué. The onion block also uses this fine-line

A dark narrow band of fabric on the pear body's right edge makes it pop out from a too-similar colored background.

appliqué shadow to make the design pop away from the background fabric. This technique is discussed in detail in Chapter 3, The Pear (see page 36).

QUILTING BASICS

Fabric and its Preparation

One hundred percent cotton with a tight weave works best. Cotton is essential if you are new to needleturn appliqué. In hand appliqué, it is common to turn under seams that are a scant 1/16". Loose weaves or high-percentage synthetic blends fray when touched with the tip of a needle.

There are two theories about washing and drying fabric. One is to never prewash. I believe this is similar to saying, "Shoot me," then hoping the gun misfires. It's a matter of time until some fabric will bleed—the smoking gun. Washing removes excess dyes, shrinks the fabric, and removes the finishing chemicals applied by the manufacturer. All in all, prewashing is a wise practice to prevent fabric bleeding and yardage that shrinks unequally when the completed quilt is washed. After your prewashed fabric is dry, iron it before cutting.

Threads

Two types of thread are used to make a quilt: One for the top's assembly, the other for quilting. Don't interchange the two.

For hand and machine sewing, use a #50 cotton-covered polyester core thread, or a good quality 100 percent polyester that is made of long staple fibers. The choice as to what brand to use is yours. My caveat is to stay away from cheap, off-brands of thread; doing so is poor economy. They

The quilt thread colors used in **What a Garden!** *quilt.*

break, get slipknotted while stitching, and fray.

For appliqué, use a color thread that matches the fabric being sewn—not the background block; for example, sew a red flower to a white background with red thread. For piecing, use a color of thread that blends best with the fabrics being joined, or choose a color that will be less obvious on the lighter fabric.

Do not use quilt thread for the top's assembly. Quilt thread is too heavy, and is used only to quilt the three-layer fabric sandwich (top, batting, and backing) together into the completed unit. Quilt thread is available in 100 percent cotton, cotton-covered polyester core, and 100 percent polyester. I prefer the polyester core thread. It has the advantage of cotton, and provides the strength and durability of polyester—which doesn't rot.

How do you choose the quilting thread color? The quilting thread color is a design decision, and best made *after* the quilt top is completed. When deciding on the quilting design, determine whether the quilting stitches should contrast the color of the background fabric, or blend in.

Color choice is also influenced by the quality of your quilting stitches. For a beginner, I recommend that the quilt thread blend with the quilt top *and* the backing fabric. The effect is the same, but uneven quilting stitches on the backing of the quilt will not be obvious. For more experienced quilters, using contrasting quilting threads adds punch. I frequently use three or more quilting thread colors to enhance the top's design.

Coating Compounds

For centuries, beeswax was a sewing basket staple. Beeswax prevents thread wear and helps eliminate slipknots. Use it to coat all threads for hand sewing. Once the thread is cut into a sewing length (no more than 18"), press it against the beeswax surface with your thumb, and pull the thread over the surface of the wax. Remove the excess by pulling the thread between thumb and index finger. Knot the thread end that was cut off at the spool, and thread the needle.

As the twentieth century ended, a new sewing product emerged to put the industrious bee out of business. Thread Heaven® replaces beeswax and goes one step further. Thread Heaven is an inert, synthetic product ("inert" means it safe for you to

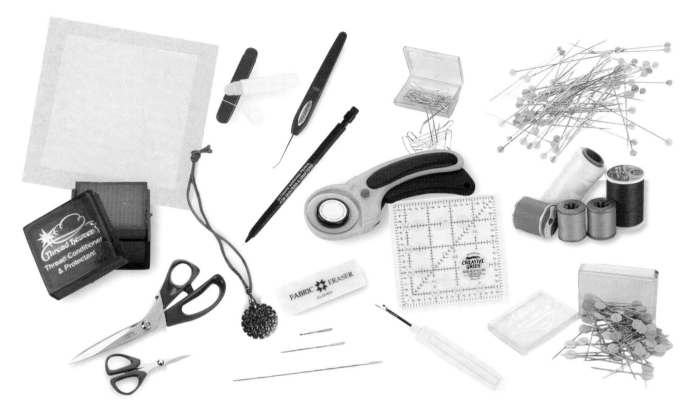

A variety of supplies used in quiltmaking.

use, and easy on the environment.) Used just like beeswax, it makes the thread glide more easily through the fabric and reduces thread fraying.

Needles

Needles are a quilter's main tool. The appropriate needle will make your stitching life easier. To make a quilt, you need only two types of needles: A Sharp for the entire assembly of the top, and a Between or Quilting needle (same needle, two names) for the quilting.

The Sharp is long, slender, and has a small

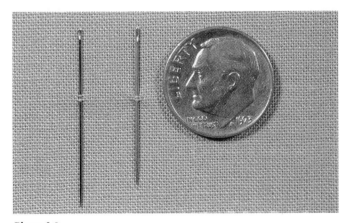

Photo I-8
A #12 Sharp needle on the left and a #10 Between on the right in comparison to a dime.

eye. The Between is short, more "fat" and has a round eye to accommodate the larger quilt thread.

Next, consider the needle sizing. Sizing is the same for both style needles; the bigger the number, the smaller and/or finer the needle. A #8 is both longer and larger in diameter than a #12. Bottom line: use the finest needle you can see to thread.

Most new quilters use a needle that is much too large. I prefer a #12 Sharp for piecing and appliqué, and a #10 Between for quilting. A #12 Between is available, but its eye is too small to insert quilt thread. Purchase needles in single-size packets; needle assortments are a waste of money. The largest needles in multi-size packets are for sewing dense fabrics, not quilt tops.

Some quilters prefer a Between for both appliqué and piecing. I find the needle shaft too short to maneuver adequately for piecing. For appliqué, I want the needle shaft to be flexible enough to glide through fabric. Frankly, it comes down to personal preference.

Thimbles

I ask two questions of new students: Who among us is left-handed, and who does not use a

Photo I-9
Thimble styles. Back row: (left to right) double-sided metal/leather, leather, and metal thimbles. Front row: Tortoise thimble, Japanese finger thimble, and square plate leather thimble.

thimble? My inquiries prove that one-third of stitchers do not or cannot stitch wearing a thimble. I fall into this latter group. Certainly, a running-stitch quilter must use a thimble or risk permanent damage to the needle-pushing finger. A punch-and-poke quilter does not need a thimble because no lateral pressure is applied to the needle. My middle finger has developed a callus for piecing and appliqué work.

Rulers

The ugly truth about measuring tools is that they may not be accurate. *What*, you ask? You thought a ruler was a ruler, or a 2" square template was really square—right? Wrong. Here is a secret experienced quilters discovered the hard way. One company's inch may not be another company's inch. That also applies to graph paper: Grids may not be square.

If you have been switching between brands of rulers and your drafted quilt patches don't fit together properly, this could be the reason. What

Important Fact

1/4" measurements may not be the same on both sides of a ruler. If there is a difference, draw an arrow with a permanent marker to the side that coincides with your benchmark measurement.

do you do? First, check all measuring tools against each other. Pick one and use it as your benchmark tool. Next, use a permanent marker and label all other rulers that do not match (or, all those that do). Now do an accuracy check with the benchmark ruler on graph paper, templates, and block patterns. Interesting, isn't it? Label them also.

This also pertains to the sewing machine. Many machines are constructed using metric measurements. Perhaps the distance between the sewing machine needle and the 1/4" mark on the presser plate do not agree with your benchmark ruler. Using an accurate 1/4" marking is useless if the same measurement is not used when machine piecing. The results are seam allowances that do not match, and finished blocks that are not the desired size.

Justifying the Ruler and Sewing Machine 1/4"

It is easy to make both your ruler and sewing machine measurements match. Draw an accurate pencil line 1/4" from the edge of a piece of white paper with the benchmark ruler. Remove the presser foot. Place the paper under the needle so that it extends in front of the needle. Hand rotate the flywheel until the needle stabs through the pencil line on the paper. Move the paper until the right edge is parallel to the feed dog slots. Tape it in place.

Butt up a ruler or straight edge guide to the right of the paper. Tape it in place.

Mark a paper with a 1/4" line drawn along its right edge. Position the paper, without the presser foot in place, and rotate the flywheel so the needle pierces the pencil line. Tape the paper's ends in place so they will not move, making sure that the paper is parallel to the side of the presser plate opening or the line will be at an angle.

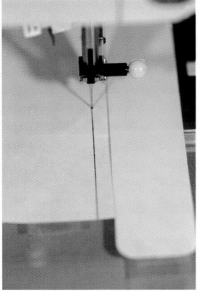

Photo I-11
Line up a ruler along the paper's edge. Tape in place and remove the paper.

Completed guidelines placed on both sides of the presser foot.

Remove the paper guide. Use a fine-line permanent marker and draw a line along the left edge of the guide (either on the body of the machine or the sewing table, depending on your machine's style). Repeat this process to the left side of the needle.

Let the ink dry. Your machine is marked with accurate 1/4" sewing guidelines on both sides of the sewing foot, and the measurements are the same as your benchmark ruler.

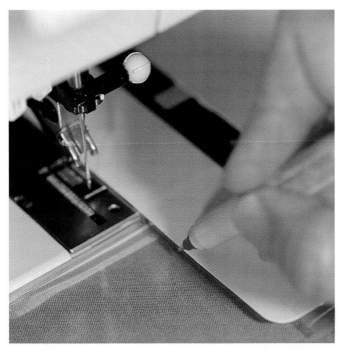

Mark a permanent parallel line on the presser plate or machine table. Repeat on the left side of the needle for 1/4" seam lines on either side of the needle.

Caution
This is a permanent line. A cotton swab moistened with alcohol can remove some of the line, but a stain could remain. Use pencil first, making sure that the lines are parallel. Decide if you want a permanent line.

Hint
Place a stack of masking tape (eight layers) or a stack of Post-It Notes™ along the ink line as a fabric bumper when stitching. This is an especially good technique to teach children to sew a straight line.

PIECING BASICS
Each template pattern is marked with a straight-of-grain arrow. To avoid stretching the fabric when piecing or pressing the fabric, line up the arrow on the fabric's straight-of-grain before cutting the patches. Sometimes it is more important to follow the fabric design than the straight-of-grain. In that case, ignore the straight-of-grain, but use care when cutting, piecing, and pressing to maintain accurate patch dimensions because bias-edged patches stretch.

The large background blocks can be pieced by hand or machine. Seam allowances for all piecing are 1/4". Seam allowances *are not* included unless specifically mentioned. You add accurate 1/4" seams using your own benchmark ruler and sewing machine measurements. (See Rulers, page 12.)

Seam Allowance Rules

❖ Hand piecing: The stitching line is marked onto the wrong side of the fabric with a fine-pointed pencil (see Chapter 2, page 36). The cutting line is not important in hand piecing. An approximate 1/4" wide seam allowance is cut.

❖ Machine piecing: Seam allowance accuracy is crucial. A 1/4" seam width is included whether you are rotary cutting or hand cutting.

❖ Needleturn appliqué: Accurate seam allowances are not essential—about 1/4". It is necessary to include enough seam allowance when cutting so that the appliqué patch is large enough to fold under the edges. See Chapter 2, The Flower (page 36), for the basics.

❖ Fused appliqué: The patches are machine zig-zagged in place with this technique. Add seam allowances that are *less wide* than the machine zigzag stitch; this allows the seam allowance to fall under the stitching so that the raw edges are completely covered.

❖ Buttonhole appliqué: Cut out actual-sized patches and attach them to the block with either a hand or machine buttonhole stitch. Fusing is not necessary.

THE MASTER PATTERN

A Master Pattern is a real-size paper pattern without seam allowances. It is used in two ways: Transferring appliqué designs or quilting patterns to a background block. The transfer is the same technique, but the end product varies.

Advantages to Using a Master Pattern

Duplication is simple because repeat blocks are working from the same original drawing: The Master Pattern. With appliqué, there is no guesswork as to where a patch is to be sewn. Quilting patterns are easy to position and put on fabric *before* the fabric is sewn into the quilt top.

Use a Master Pattern for a sash or border designs and it will match throughout the quilt. It is easy to lay exact patterns onto multiple strips of sash or border fabric.

A pencil is used to draw the original paper Master Pattern so that corrections are made with an eraser.

Creating a Master Pattern

1. Draw an accurate block on a piece of paper. Use a standard-weight drawing paper so that it is sturdy enough to use for repeat blocks or projects. Typing or shelf paper can be taped together.

2. Cut out the paper to the finished size (no seam allowances). For example: Chapter 3, The Pear, is 12" square. Ignore the fact that the block is pieced; only the appliqué design is important.

3. Draw light diagonal pencil lines on the paper block from corner to corner to locate its exact center.

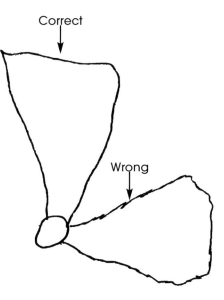

Illus. I-2
The single lines of the top leaf will not show when an appliqué patch is sewn. The leaf's lines on the right are uneven and will show when an appliqué patch is in place.

Completed master pattern. Notice that the lines are single, in black permanent ink.

4. Overlay the paper onto the pear design or work with a photocopy of the design, so that the center of the paper block overlays the dashed lines in the center of the pear's body.

5. Trace over the entire design using a mechanical pencil. Draw so that the lines are smooth and make a single, thin line. Do not scratch pencil lines back and forth. It helps to rest the heel of your hand on the paper and use it as a pivot point in order to draw accurate curves and straight lines.

6. Once all pencil lines are exact, re-mark them using a fine point, black, felt-tipped pen. DO NOT use a ballpoint pen, as it could leave globs of ink that will transfer to fabric. Once the lines are completed in ink, erase all pencil lines. The Master Pattern is ready to use.

7. With the Master Pattern right side up, pin a fabric block over it with the fabric right side up.

8. Scotch tape the entire unit to a window-pane or lay it over a light box. The black felt-tipped pattern lines will be visible, even through a dark background fabric.

Transferring a master pattern to the right side of a background block.

9. Trace over all lines with a mechanical pencil. DO NOT use a water-soluble pen. Only press hard enough to make a fine, light, single pencil line on the right side of the fabric. DO NOT scratch back and forth. These lines on the fabric are the appliqué stitching lines or the stitching lines for a quilt pattern. It is difficult to determine if you are pressing hard enough as you trace because the drawing is directly over a black line. To see if the pencil line is dark enough, slip your hand between the fabric and Master Pattern. There is a fine line, no pun intended, between too light and too dark. Lift the pencil off the fabric every 2" or so to allow the fabric to settle in place. Continue until the entire design is transferred to the background block.

10. The prepared block is now ready for appliqué by hand or machine or, if it is a sash or border quilt pattern, to be joined into the quilt top.

The completed Master Pattern transferred onto a background block.

IMPORTANT INFORMATION

❖ DO NOT USE a blue washable fabric marker. Even after it is washed out, hot water brings the marks back, which can be set *permanently*. A hot iron does the same thing.

❖ Don't agonize over color selection. Let yourself go. Expand your horizons with vibrant colors and unexpected combinations. When studying my photographs taken at the International Quilt Festival in Houston, Texas, I discovered something unexpected: Hot, vibrantly colored quilts. I had taken photos of what I really preferred. Thus, the **What a Garden!** color scheme was born. Those photographs made me realize how my color sense has evolved. I let myself go when choosing fabric for the **What a Garden!** quilt, introducing bold fabrics to the end. It is my favorite of the two quilts.

❖ A variety of solid colors or prints can be used for background blocks, but a background fabric's design should not overwhelm the appliquéd designs.

❖ Perhaps muted or pastel colors are your choice. There is no right or best way to reach your final selections. That makes the creation exciting.

❖ A dark blue or black background and brilliant appliqué colors will create a quilt with a contemporary look. Visualize a black background and appliqués made with multiple black and white fabrics.

❖ The blocks are in an order so that the easiest appliqués come in the first chapters and the most challenging toward the last.

❖ Practice does make perfect.

❖ When all the blocks are completed, you will be accomplished at needleturn or machine appliqué.

Hand and Machine Appliqué, Fusing, and Freezer Paper Appliqué

DECIDING ON TECHNIQUES

As you contemplate beginning the **Savory Garden** quilt, the first decision is whether to use hand or machine appliqué exclusively or combine several techniques. There is no single or best method, only what works for you and the individual project. Time or personal preference may be crucial in opting for machine work. The appearance of the end product could be more important. For instance, a set of kitchen curtains that have to stand up to light and frequent washing dictate machine appliqué.

For many, the thought of hand appliquéing an entire quilt signals an imminent panic attack. If you fall in this not-in-my-lifetime group, reconsider and try needleturn appliqué guided by the close-up photography and detailed directions. Most of my students may not become full-fledged converts, but overcome their fear of turning under fabric raw edges with a needle while sewing to a pencil line. Hand appliquéing allows you to get it done at the doctor's office, baseball bleachers, or when traveling. Hand appliqué is a truly portable technique.

Additionally, there are other methods of appliqué. All have their advantages and drawbacks. Study the examples in this chapter, and determine which method appeals to you then perfect that technique. Remember, several appliqué options can be combined.

TRANSFERRING A PATTERN TO THE BACKGROUND FABRIC: MASTER PATTERN, VINYL OVERLAY, PLUNK AND PIN

❖ Master Pattern: This is a full-sized pattern without seam allowances that is drawn onto a paper template with a pencil. I recommend making two duplicates. It may require taping two pages together for the complete pattern. Keep the first one as an original, and to lay the Master Pattern on the background block; cut up the other for patterns.

❖ The completed Master Pattern is placed, face up, and a background block is pinned right-side-up, over the Master Pattern. The pinned unit is taped to a window or placed over a light box. The pattern lines will be clearly visible. Trace over each line with a mechanical pencil marking a single, fine, *light* line. *Do not scratch back and forth* (see Introduction: Illus. I-2, page 14). These are the appliqué sewing lines. The background block is ready for appliqué.

❖ Vinyl overlay: This method finds the correct sewing location for a patch without laying a pencil line onto the background block. The real-size pattern is applied to a clear vinyl sheet with a black permanent marker. The

Photo 1-1
The appliqué pattern is transferred to vinyl and then basted to the top of the background block. The patch is moved until positioned correctly, and the vinyl is flipped out of the way for sewing. It remains attached for the duration of the block's appliqué.

Photo 1-2
"Plunk and pin" means the pattern is referred to and the patch's location is "eyeballed" into position for appliqué.

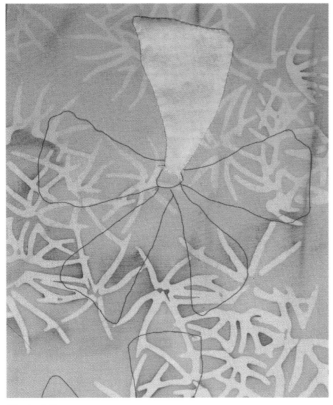

Photo 1-3
An upper portion of a background block with the Master Pattern in pencil and one patch sewn on with needleturn appliqué.

vinyl sheet is basted to the top edge of the background block. It stays attached until the appliqué is completed. When a patch needs to be applied, the vinyl is dropped over the right side of the background block. The patch is placed under it, and shifted about until it is in its correct position and pinned in place. The vinyl sheet is flipped out of the way, and appliqué proceeds using any technique. When the entire design is completed, the vinyl pattern is removed.

❖ Plunk & Pin: A variety of sewing techniques can be used, but this method creates a design location problem since there is no pattern on the background block. The stitcher refers to the original pattern for placement guidance and moves the fabric patches on the background fabric until pleased with the arrangement. The patches are pinned in place and appliquéd. While this method works for a single block, it is difficult to duplicate exact patch placement on multiple blocks.

HAND METHODS OF APPLIQUÉ: NEEDLETURN AND BASTING

❖ Needleturn using a Master Pattern, block preparation: For hand sewing, the background block is marked with the finished-size seam lines on the wrong side of the fabric using a pencil. The block is cut 1/4" outside the pencil lines, which leaves seam allowances on all edges. For machine sewing, the background block is rotary cut to the desired size including the 1/4" seam allowance. After the Master Pattern is marked, each appliqué patch is cut out with seam allowances, and placed on the Master Pattern, right side up, positioned so there is ample seam allowance on all edges, then pinned or glue-basted in place. The excess fabric seam allowance is trimmed just before being turned under by the needle, not the fingers. The patch is sewn to the pencil lines on the background block with an almost invisible stitch. This leaves the appliqué fabric floating as a separate layer above the background block, creating dimension. No basting is required. Each succeeding chapter will cover specific techniques in detail.

❖ Basting: Each patch is cut out, and seam allowances are turned under and basted in place before appliqué begins. There are two drawbacks with this method. Basting should be made of long stitches, but basting a curve requires short stitches or points will form on the fabric's edge. Using tiny basting stitches followed by the appliqué means detail stitching is done twice. If the patch is ironed after basting … yikes! The errors are set in and almost impossible to remove when the patch is being appliquéd down.

❖ Buttonhole Stitch: This embroidery handwork is done over the edge of the patch to encase the raw edges. The raw edges will be visible under the buttonhole work. I prefer a turned-under seam allowance so there is no chance of raveling. First, a narrow seam allowance is folded under on the seam line and held in place with a small running stitch using a matching color of thread. The patch is then buttonholed down. The running stitch thread remains.

MACHINE APPLIQUÉ: FUSING, FREEZER PAPER, PAPER STABILIZERS

❖ Machine appliqué: The appliqué patch edges are attached by sewing machine. The stitching can be straight line, an open zigzag, satin stitch, or a decorative stitch pattern. The patch is held in place with pins, glue-basted, or fused down prior to stitching.

❖ Fusing: A variety of products glue-fuse a fabric patch to the background block. This turns two fabrics into one and makes the design area stiff. While the patch edges may not ravel, there is no dimension with this technique and edges can pull up when washed. Hand stitching is difficult through fused fabric. Regardless of the

Photo 1-4
Two samples of basted patches using large stitches on the left and tiny basting on floral petal curves.

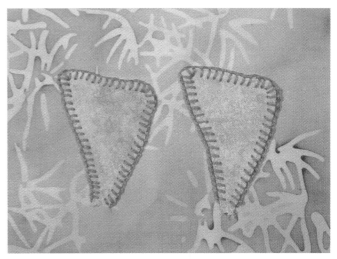

Photo 1-5
Raw-edge buttonhole on the left and turned-edge buttonhole on the right. Notice how the edges are much smoother when the edges are basted under prior to buttonhole stitching.

Photo 1-6
A quick sample of possible machine appliqué stitches. Some are not appropriate because the fabric edges are not covered or the turn corners smooth.

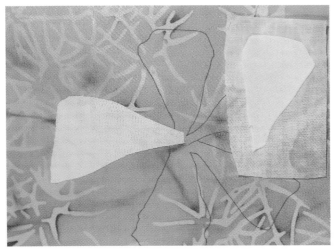

Photo 1-7
The patch on the right shows the fusing paper attached to the wrong side of the fabric. The patch on the left is fused to the background fabric. Notice the seam allowance only extends into the flower's center.

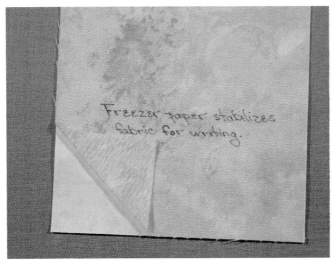

Photo 1-8
Freezer paper is easily removed after being pressed onto fabric. It leaves no residue and stabilizes fabric for printing.

Photo 1-9
Regular paper leaves small bits under the stitching line that are difficult to remove.

problems, it is a popular, fast technique. Fusing allows incorporation of tiny curves along the edge of the design where it might not be possible with traditional needleturn or basting techniques. The sample is cut without seam allowances, except where the petal extends under the flower's center.

❖ Freezer paper: Reynolds® Freezer Paper is sold in the grocery store and is intended for wrapping food products for a home freezer. When it is ironed onto fabric, its plastic coating forms a temporary bond with the fabric—making it stiff. The paper pulls off with no change to the fabric. The paper allows the fabric to be manipulated in a variety of ways. A true-size template can be ironed to the right side of the fabric and the seam allowances folded under and stitched in place. It can be ironed to the wrong side of the fabric and the seam allowances pressed under. This method can result in unwanted points forming and scorched fingers. It can be ironed to background blocks that are then run through a computer printer to transfer designs to the right side of the fabric; *check the printer manufacturer's recommendations before trying this.* It can be pressed on the wrong side of fabric to stabilize it for handwriting.

❖ Paper Stabilizers: There are a variety of tear-away papers or synthetic products for stabilizing fabric to prevent it from stretching during the machine appliqué process. The ability to remove the stabilizer after the stitching is completed should determine its usage. With typing paper, examining table paper, or freezer paper, stitches should be short: 25 to 30 per inch so that the paper separates easily for removal. Tearing the paper away so that the machine stitching is not distorted is the first problem. When using a dense stitching pattern, a narrow strip of paper remains under the thread and results in a rigid area. Trying to pick it out with tweezers is a nightmare.

WATER SOLUBLE STABILIZERS

Water soluble stabilizers completely disappear when plunged in water. Solvy™ looks like a clear plastic wrap and comes in a variety of weights. YLI Wash-A-Way Paper™ is a lightweight 8" x 11-1/2" paper sheet. The paper is opaque enough that the pattern can be seen from both sides. This means that the pattern does not have to be reversed for paper piecing, which is a definite advantage. The YLI Wash-A-Way Paper can also be put through a printer to create a pattern. Once stitching is completed the fabric is plunged in water. The paper dissolves almost immediately. There is no fabric distortion. Both products can be drawn upon.

Photo 1-10
Solvy™ stitched to the back of the block as a stabilizer.

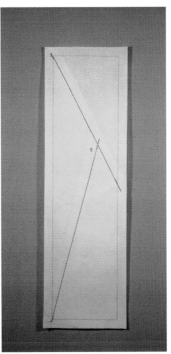

Photo 1-12
YLI Wash-A-Way Paper used as a stabilizer/paper piecing foundation for piecing a block.

Photo 1-11
Running water dissolves Solvy™.

Photo 1-13
Running water dissolves Wash-A-Way Paper.

COMPARISON OF STITCHING METHODS

Study the photographs for hand, machine, and fusing. There is no single best way to appliqué; it is a matter of preference, and how you want the finished product to look and feel. Realize that fusing turns two fabrics into one and, until better products are available, makes it stiff.

Time Versus Technique

While time is a critical factor in quiltmaking, accuracy is still paramount. No one wants a quilt that billows out from the wall or ripples across a bed like waves on the ocean. This means that it is crucial you take the time to make accurate templates, cut blocks that are faithful to the pattern's measurements, and sew exact 1/4" seams. The payoffs are square corners, smooth borders, and flat bindings. Another benefit is that it takes less time to make an accurate quilt than to force inexact pieces to fit in place.

There is no single best technique for making a quilt. When I began quilting in 1975, I worked by hand because I liked the control and the accurate results I got when piecing or appliquéing. While my love of handwork is as strong as ever, time and pressure to produce samples have made me search for faster production methods to get the same results. I now use a combination of hand and machine work, melding the two together in a smooth fashion. This affords me the speed of machine sewing blocks, sashing, borders, and binding while employing the portability of appliqué and piecing to appease my need for handwork. I also keep a project close by that is portable, ready to go as I head out the door. All of the blocks from the **Savory Garden** patterns lend themselves to this grab-and-run philosophy. Whether you appliqué during a coffee break or piece a block while waiting to see a doctor, it is up to you to decide when to use each technique depending upon your available time.

Consider, too, the quilt's intended use. A quilt for a child's bed may be loved into oblivion while a cherished wedding quilt lasts for generations. Your vision, available time, developing skills, and needs working together will dictate which techniques you choose to make the **Savory Garden** quilt.

YARDAGE REQUIREMENTS

Specific appliqué yardage is discussed in each of the block's chapters. However, most appliqué designs will use no more than a fat quarter (18" x 22" piece of fabric) of any fabric and many will require a lot less. It also depends on how many times the same fabric is repeated. Scraps and a nice fabric stash will probably be adequate.

The background fabric yardage can also vary depending on how many fabrics are used. The traditional colored **Savory Garden** quilt used only one fabric for the background. The **What a Garden!** background uses three fabrics: Light green batik, a grayed soft plaid, and a strong teal tone-on-tone dot. It may appear that more fabrics were used, but this is the advantage of a multicolored batik—many looks can come from one length of yardage. The brick blocks and borders also use three fabrics. If using traditional prints, I suggest a minimum of five, possibly seven or nine prints, to create enough visual interest and the look of a random arrangement.

YARDAGE REQUIREMENTS

Background blocks: 3-1/4 yards (allows for shrinkage)
Main color: 2 yds
Bricks: 3 colors, 1/4 to 3-1/4 yd each, depending on the number of fabrics
Backing: 3-1/3 yds if pieced across the quilt width (leaves a 22" x 59" strip leftover to use in piecing, or 3-2/3 yards if pieced the length of the quilt (leaves a 29" x 66" strip leftover to use in piecing)
Binding: 2/3 yard for strips cut 2-1/2" wide. Quilt requires 7 yds of binding. It is not cut on the bias, but cut across the width of the 44"-wide fabric. Leftover backing could be used for the binding.

These are the appliqué fabrics used in the **What a Garden!** *quilt.*

The background fabrics.

ADDITIONAL THOUGHTS

View each quilt as a new road to an exciting creation. Don't be locked into a single quilt technique or typical color combinations. Make the **Savory Garden** quilt your breakout piece. Select electrifying, nontraditional colors. This could mean using a hot fuchsia batik instead of a pastel pink print.

Study your quilt photographs to see if they are telling you something surprising about color. Which quilt stopped you dead in your tracks at a quilt show? Determine what is striking about a quiltmaker's combination of prints and colors. Are unusual tones laid side-by-side? Are prints and plaids your mother said would never go together pleasing to your eye? Be daring, be brave, and make your next shopping excursion a fabric journey.

Try new techniques, and persist until you feel comfortable doing them. Remember, when you learn anything for the first time it is work. You are so focused on learning and getting it right that the sheer enjoyment of the process is lost. But once technique is learned, the fun begins.

Above all, don't be afraid to make mistakes. I view each quilt as a learning experience: Finding a new technique, perfecting a fabric point, placing an unusual print in a creative way or blending colors into a new pallet.

What if something does not turn out the way you intended? Relax. Enjoy what you have done, and plan your next quilt project.

View the variety of techniques that are covered in the succeeding chapters as a trip into a land of exciting color concoctions and challenging techniques. Unearth new favorites while expanding your talents, realizing that there is no single best way to do everything. That is what keeps quiltmakers so enthused. Different choices for different quilters, and at different times for different projects.

An unborn quilt is waiting for you to put newly found expertise into practice. Now, go create the **Savory Garden** with your unique interpretation.

chapter 2

The Flower

COLOR AND TECHNIQUE CHOICES

Flamboyant or traditional, wild or muted … it is time to decide which fabrics to use to create your unique quilt. Study the color selections in both sample quilts. (See Photos 1-1 and 1-2.) Because the traditionally colored quilt is more straightforward, the **What a Garden!** quilt is used throughout the book as an example. Each chapter begins with two photographs: The completed block and the fabrics used, followed by a line drawing of the block with patch numbers and yardage amounts.

Photo 2-1
*The **What a Garden!** quilt uses flamboyant colors and is featured in each chapter.*

Flower Yardage
Background block: 12-1/2" x 16-1/2"
(cut size, seams included)
Stems and leaves: narrow strips,
(each no longer than 2" x 11")
Flower center: 3" square
Flower: 1/4 yd or a fat quarter

The fabrics used in the flower.

Multi-colored fabrics and batiks were selected for the **What a Garden!** designs so that color variations were possible using fewer fabrics. For example, only three fabrics are used for the bricks: A water spot brown/lavender and two batiks, a gold-brown and a brown with rust and darker brown. The background uses three fabrics that add textural interest, but don't overwhelm the appliqué designs: A light green batik, a soft faux-green and a single use of a muted lime green to add punch in the pear block. This single-use of the lime green fabric would be repeated more times throughout the piecing if the quilt was remade. Keep this in mind when living with your color choices. Fabric selection and placement may not be wrong, but there are always other options. Color in the schematic to

block in color options for the background.

Needleturn appliqué is a matter of learning how to control fabric and turning under narrow seam allowances smoothly. The more deep a curve, the narrower its seam allowance must be. The knack is to create smooth edges without unwanted points or uneven stitching. Whether you are a beginner or more advanced quilter, learning new techniques can be daunting. That is why this chapter begins with the most basic shapes: Cutting out the background block and appliquéing gentle curved edges, easy arcs, and a large circle. Later on in the chapter, there is an option that will give a stuffed (trapunto) look to the flower design.

Illus. 2-1
The schematic of the entire quilt. Make multiple copies and color the backgrounds and designs to try different color placements before buying fabric.

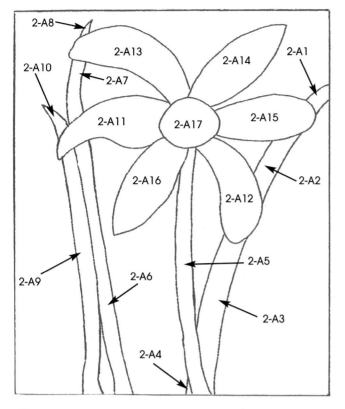

Illus. 2-2
The flower schematic.

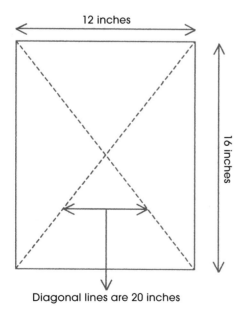

12 inches

16 inches

Diagonal lines are 20 inches

Illus. 2-3
The flower background block measures 12" x 16", finished size.
Diagonal measurements of 20" means it is square.

The Background Block

The first step is to make a template that will perform dual duty as a pattern for cutting the background block and as a master pattern for the appliqué design. The finished block size is 12" x 16". Typing or graph paper can be taped together to get the correct size. To eliminate taped seams, use large sheets of graph, shelf, or drawing paper. It is essential that the rectangle be accurate. This is easy to do when applying the time-honored carpenter's trick of checking diagonal measurements: Diagonal lines are the same length, assuring that any rectangle or square is square. The diagonal measurement for a 12" x 16" rectangle is 20".

Use this rectangular template for making the Master Pattern following the directions in the Introduction (see Introduction: Master Pattern). Center the design and align the corner block registration marks. Once the Master Pattern is complete, with all the Flower's pattern lines marked with a fine-line, black, felt-tipped pen, cut out the background block either for hand or machine piecing. For hand piecing, mark the 12" x 16" rectangle onto the wrong side of the fabric with a mechanical pencil. This is the block's stitching line for sewing it into the quilt top. Cut out the block 1/4" *outside* the pencil lines on all edges. (See ALERT before cutting.) This creates a 1/4" seam allowance. For machine piecing, *include* a 1/4" measurement (12-1/2" x 16-1/2") on all edges when making the Master Pattern for rotary cutting. Next, pin the right side of the Master Pattern to the wrong side of the fabric. Flower head pins work the best since they lay flat and do not distort the fabric—but they are not essential. Tape the entire unit to a window or lay it on a light box, and trace over each pattern line onto the *right side* of the fabric using a mechanical pencil. See Introduction, Master Pattern, for detailed instructions. The background block is ready for appliqué.

ALERT

Fabric edges fray during the appliqué process. Avoid raveling into the 1/4" seam allowances by cutting the appliqué block seam allowances 1/2" wide and trim down after the appliqué is completed.

Cutting the Fabric Patches

Each template is cut individually from a paper pattern that is traced or photocopied from the original pattern. It is not necessary to use Mylar for appliqué templates since each design is used only once. To avoid confusion, be sure to label each paper shape with its number. (See the Introduction, Pattern Numbering, page 8.) Whether or not you will include seam allowances depends on the method you choose to do the appliqué. Review the Introduction, Piecing Basics, for more detail.

Seam Allowance Requirements

Needleturn appliqué
Add 1/4" seam allowances

Fused appliqué
Add 1/4" seams only where the patch is covered by another appliqué; otherwise, there are no seam allowances.
Buttonhole appliqué
No seams allowances unless the edges are to be folded and basted under prior to stitching and/or where covered by another patch.

APPLIQUÉ FUNDAMENTALS

Regardless of which appliqué technique you use, start appliquéing the most distant patch and build toward the foreground. In The Flower, this is the sequence: leaves, stem, flower petals and flower center. Pattern pieces are numbered in the sewing sequence. Begin with 2-A1 and work to the final number, 2-A17.

Each long leaf could be cut from a single piece of fabric. However, that will mean the petals will be sewn over portions of the leaves. This will work in some instances, but it poses two questions. Is the bottom fabric darker than the top fabric? Will it be visible through the covering appliqué fabric? These are determining factors in overlaying fabrics. If the under fabric could show, use short segments rather than whole pieces.

Layering Appliqué Fabrics and Quilting

Though the quilting process is far in the future, consider it before appliqué begins if you plan to quilt within the appliqué shapes to create added dimension. Machine quilting is not an issue, as quilting through multiple layers of fabric is easy. A punch and poke quilter will have little difficulty because the needle is poked through the fabric at a perpendicular angle. However, a running-stitch quilter will encounter a problem. Moving the needle through stacked layers of appliqué at an oblique angle (when quilting the more complex designs, especially the onion, asparagus, peas and peppers), is challenging. To compensate for this, cut away the multiple layers after the appliqué is completed to eliminate fabric bulk.

A Word about Beginning and Ending Thread

Throughout the assembly of the quilt, whether appliquéing, piecing, or quilting, use only a single strand of thread. Doubling the thread will cause stiffer seams, and history has proven that a single thread is sufficient. Sewing with longer thread lengths creates slipknots, thread snarls, and excessive wearing of the thread, so cut it no more than 18". Make a small knot at the end of the thread that was cut from the spool. There are many ways to make a knot; I loop it around my index finger and roll it with my thumb until a small knot forms, then pull it tight.

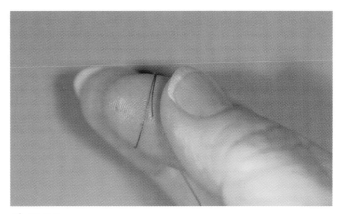

Photo 2-3
There are many ways to create a thread knot. Here, the thread is rolled between thumb and forefinger to form a knot.

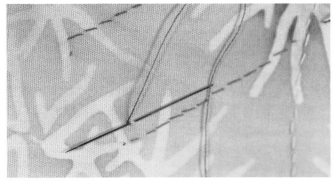

Photo 2:4
To begin the figure-8 knot, run the needle under the appliqué or in the stitching line for piecing and picking up a few threads of the fabric.

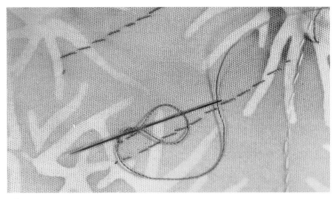

Photo 2:5
Pull the thread through to form a loop and twist it into a figure-8. Run the needle through the top figure-8 loop and out the bottom. Pull it snug to the fabric.

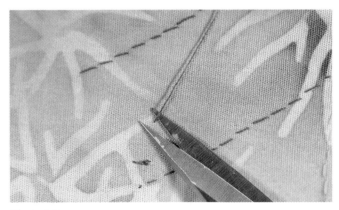

Photo 2-6
Run the needle between the fabric layers and cut the thread.

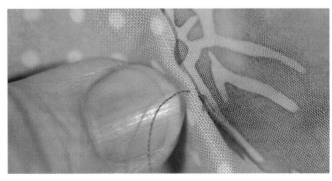

Photo 2-7
Place the knot under the edge of the appliqué, not the background block.

Ending the thread so that the knot does not come undone is critical. There is no single way to make an ending knot, but it must be secure. I use a figure-8 method for both hand appliqué and piecing. First, pick up several threads of the background fabric about 1/8" to 1/4" inside the appliqué area (or within the stitching line if piecing).

Pull the thread though until it forms a dime-size loop. The thread may have already twisted into a figure-8. If not, use the needle and twist the thread to make one. Put the needle through the top loop and out the bottom loop, aiming the needle toward the fabric. Pull the thread through the loops, and slowly tighten until the knot is snug against the fabric. Hold your thumbnail against the thread and pull the knot tight—don't miss this step. If it is not tightened down, the knot can come undone.

Run the needle between the background block and the appliqué and bring it out the background block about 1/4" away so the thread tail is captured between the layers, or leave a 1/4" tail when piecing.

The Appliqué Stitch

The appliqué stitch is simple. It is used for all appliqué, and stitching the folded edge of the binding to the completed quilt. To begin, cut a thread 12" to 18", apply thread coating, and knot the end cut from the spool. Bring the needle under the appliqué patch so the knot rests at the edge of the turned-under seam allowance.

Poke the needle into the background block *directly* opposite of where the thread comes out of the appliqué fabric—*this is important, otherwise the thread will be visible.* Bring the needle forward 1/8" to 1/4", determined by the shape of the appliqué, and run it back out until it just catches the edge of the appliqué. Pull the thread snug, and keep repeating the stitch until the appliqué is attached. That's it!

Notice that the two stitches in Photo 2-9 are taken into the background ahead or behind where the thread comes out of the appliqué. The stitches lay on the surface and are obvious.

Needleturning the Seam Allowance

Needleturn is named correctly. It means that fingers do not; I repeat, *do not* turn the seam allowance under. The needle manipulates the fabric so that the seam allowance rolls under the body of the appliqué patch onto the Master Pattern pencil line. The thread is started and the needle tip pokes into the seam allowance about an inch in front of where the thread comes out the appliqué. Pull the needle back toward the appliqué thread. The seam allowance will roll under right onto the pencil line just like magic. Hold the edge with your thumbnail and stitch that area. Repeat needle-turning in one-inch increments. See below for trimming specific areas.

Checking for Proper Thread Tension

You followed the directions, but your stitches show too much and the appliqué looks sloppy or it is rippled. What's wrong? Probably the thread's stitch tension is off. It is easy to see if the thread is pulled too tight. The background block and perhaps the appliqué are puckered. Correct it by not pulling so firmly on the thread. If you took several stitches before pulling the thread through, it causes uneven stitch tension. Pull the thread through after each stitch. It is not as noticeable if the thread is too loose. The appliqué fabric may pull away from the Master Pattern pencil line even though it is stitched right on it. Or, perhaps the stitches show too much. Slip the needle's tip under a stitch and pull up. If a loop of excess thread forms, it means the thread is not tight enough. It must be pulled so that the patch's edge is held firmly in place just short of puckering the fabric. Notice how the threads on either side of the red loop in Photo 2-11 have disappeared with proper tension.

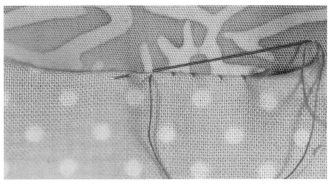

Photo 2-8
Stitch directly into the background block opposite where the thread comes out of the appliqué fabric.

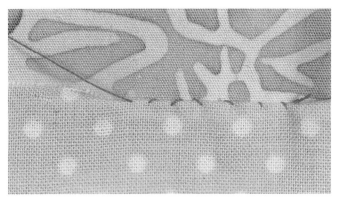

Photo 2-9
The two stitches in the middle go into the background block ahead of where the thread comes out of the appliqué patch. On the left, they go behind the thread. Both are too visible. The two stitches on the right are correct.

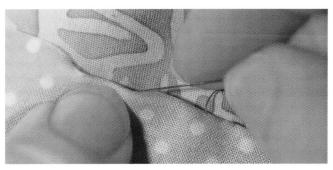

Photo 2-10
About an inch in front of the thread, poke into the seam allowance, push it under to the Master Pattern pencil line and pull the needle back towards the stitching. The seam will roll under and turn right onto the pencil line.

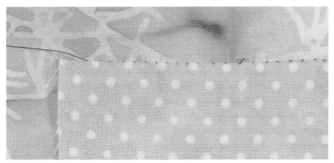

Photo 2-11
Thread tension is too tight on the left, and too loose on the far right. The tension is correct on both sides of the loop; the stitching is almost invisible.

Photo 2-12
The heart shows stitch lengths of straight and curved areas of 1/4" on the left and 1/8" on the right, packed together at the depth of the "V."

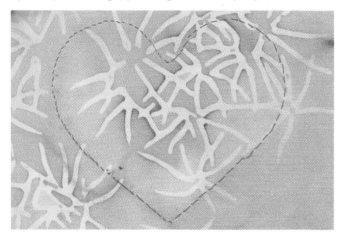

Photo 2-13
The reverse side of the appliqué shows variations in the stitch length. The red dot is the ending knot.

Photo 2-14
When a portion of an appliqué patch is covered by another patch, baste the raw edge in place within the seam allowance.

Photo 2-15
Trim as you go. It is a recipe for disaster to trim too far ahead. Eventually, a patch will come up too short and will have to be redone.

Stitch Length

For beginning appliquérs, the stitch length should be less than 1/4" in a straight area. If longer, the appliqué fabric gaps along the edges. In all the close-up samples in the **What a Garden!** quilt, stitch length is usually a generous 1/8". While there are few complex designs in this book, the general appliqué rule is that the tighter a curve or more complex the design, the closer the stitches must be placed. At a deep "V," it is necessary to pack the stitches so they touch to prevent fraying, as there is almost no seam allowance.

The First Stitch

Where do you start an appliqué? The answer is simple. Begin on the straightest area, but never at the depth or height of a curve, or on a point. If the patch runs off into the seam allowance (see Flower, Patch 2-1), begin stitching in the seam allowance. For a circle, start anywhere.

What if one portion of a patch covers another? It is not necessary to turn the seam allowance under and butt the edges that touch. Simply leave the raw edges of the bottom patch extended and cover it with the top patch. Tack that under-seam allowance to the background block with a small running stitch.

Trimming Seam Allowances

Seam allowances for straight-sided appliqué can remain at 1/4". However, any deviance from a straight seam requires that the 1/4" seams be trimmed down so that the fabric will fold under without ripples. *Do not* trim seam allowances more than 1" in front of where you are appliquéing. Doing so is a recipe for disaster. At some point you will have trimmed too much and will need to start over.

A Pinning Option

A frequent complaint about appliqué is that the appliqué thread tangles around pins. Here is a gluing option that eliminates pin usage: Roxanne's Glue-Baste-It™. I find it to be strong and easily removed when the piece is washed. Unlike glue sticks that have to be smeared across the fabric, this product requires only a tiny dot—smaller than a glass pinhead. Placing several glue dots *within the body of the patch* allows manipulation of the appliqué edges and does not interfere with the stitching. There is a side benefit. Fabric patches can slip out of place when appliquéing because of sideways finger pressure. The glue holds the patch so that this does not happen. To glue, place the patch over the design area, right side up, positioned so that there is sufficient seam allowance on all sides. Fold one half of the patch back. Place several glue dots up the center of the patch. If necessary, turn the patch back the other direction and repeat for the remaining half. Gently press in place and let the glue dry for a few minutes before handling.

Points

A sharp point requires trimming a lot of fabric. Tighter fabric weaves work best. They fray less and can be manipulated without disintegrating when touched with the needle's tip. First, stitch right up to the point. Take a final stitch at the exact pencil point. Flip the patch open, and trim the turned-under seam allowance to 1/8" or less, depending on the sharpness of the point.

Next, use the point of the needle to push the seam allowance back into itself. The fabric should be folded all the way back into the seam allowance, not between the background fabric and seam allowance.

Place your thumbnail over the pencil line and trim the seam allowance so that it will roll under with minimum bulk. The amount to trim depends on the angle of the point, the thickness of the fabric and how much it ravels. If the point is too bulky, open it up and trim some more. Forming fine, sharp points requires practice.

Photo 2-16
Glue basting in the center of an appliqué patch is fast, effective, and eliminates pinning.

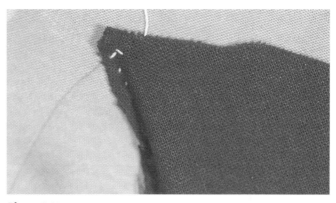

Photo 2-17
Flip the patch open and trim the seam allowance about 1/8" from the stitching line.

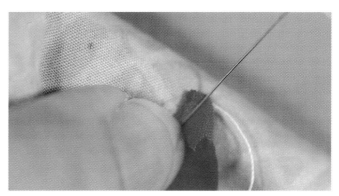

Photo 2-18
Trim the seam and push the excess between the seam allowance's fold.

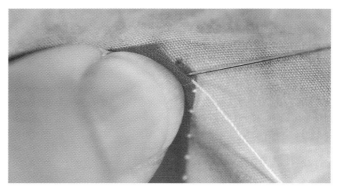

Photo 2-19
Use the needle, not fingers, to push the fabric back to form the end of the point.

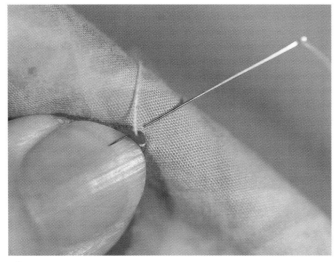

Photo 2-20
Take another stitch right into the point. It needs to be "nailed" in place to prevent raveling.

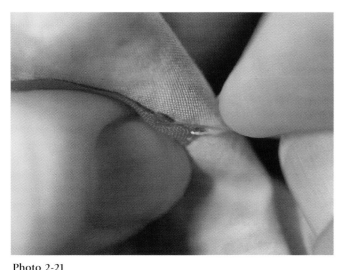

Photo 2-21
Use the side of the needle and push/force the fabric under. Do not fiddle with it too much or it will fray and become unworkable.

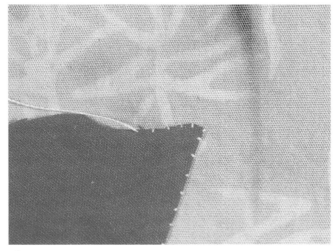

Photo 2-22
A completed point using contrasting thread for clarity.

Take another stitch right into the point. It needs to be nailed in place. Pull the thread until it is taut.

Push the trimmed seam allowance with the side of the needle and force it under. Stitch close at the point and continue stitching close together about four stitches. Continue appliquéing the patch in place.

Large Circles

The circle that forms the flower's center is not difficult, but narrower seam allowances, 1/8" or less, are required to have the edge's roll under without rippling. For a true circle, begin stitching at any location, or on a straighter edge if you are working with an oval. Shorten stitch spacing so the edge does not pucker between them. If necessary, tiny "V" shapes can be cut out of the seam allowance so that it folds under smoothly.

An Easy Option to Create Dimension

Traditional Italian trapunto (stuffed work), is done by cutting an opening into the back of the area that needs dimension, poking extra stuffing in and whipstitching the cut closed. There is an easier way to create the same effect. Once the block's design is completed, cut out a piece of batting using the pattern templates for the area to be stuffed. In the sample, I chose to stuff only the flower's petals and its center. Batting selection depends on how the finished trapunto area is to look. For more loft, use

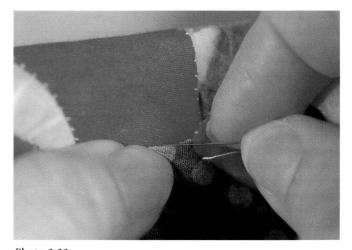

Photo 2-23
Circles require narrower seams and closer stitches. Here the fabric is being rolled under with the side of the needle.

Photo 2-24
One hundred percent cotton batting is used for this trapunto.

the extra batting and create additional height. It is also much easier to quilt without additional layers. Not everything should have dimension. Perhaps choose only the flowers or just their centers. Or, add to the round appearance of the onion, bundle of asparagus or peppers by adding stuffing only behind their center patches. Certainly, the peas could be stuffed. The key to good stuffed work is scattering it throughout the entire quilt's design area. Do not distort the shapes so it appears as if hot dogs were shoved under the patches! In this instance, less is better.

ADDITIONAL THOUGHTS

Now that the first lesson in needleturn appliqué is completed … relax. You have learned all the basics of needleturn appliqué. All the new hand techniques and more complex designs introduced in later chapters are built on what is in this chapter. No matter whether you use true needleturn, freezer paper, work with a Master Pattern or plastic overlay, each new curve or point becomes easier to handle. Though you might feel overwhelmed, nothing comes without practice. Don't expect perfection or spend your time ripping out. Keep going. With each patch, stitches become more even, and needle manipulation of fabric feels more natural. It is now time to harvest the pear, incorporate machine work, and tackle new and different challenges.

polyester. Cotton batting will be flatter. Two layers of cotton batting will build extra height. Adding too much stuffing not only looks unnatural, but it also distorts the quilt's surface. Hand baste each piece of batting to the wrong side of the background block. Use a running stitch about 1/4" long, but only take a tiny bite of the background block. Do not pull the thread tight so that a depression in the batting is created.

Are you wondering why we didn't use a single of piece of batting , but cut out an entire design? The answer has to do with quilting. By allowing a tiny space between each patch, outline quilting by hand or machine will sink between

chapter 3

The Pear

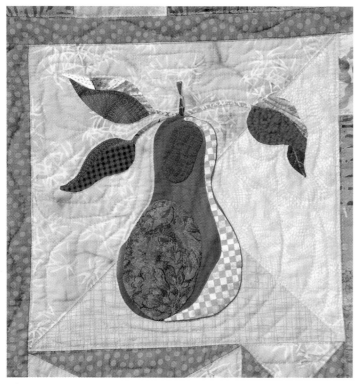

Photo 3-1
The pear.

LAYERING FABRICS

This chapter begins the technique of layering fabrics to create a shape's depth and texture. It also details needleturn appliqué, but remember, any option shown in later chapters can be used for stitching any of the designs. These options will only be discussed once.

Needleturn appliqué is a matter of learning how to control fabric and turn under narrow seam allowances so that it does not fray. As mentioned before, the more deep a curve, the narrower its seam allowance. The objective is to have smooth edges without points or uneven bulges, no matter which sewing technique is used for appliqué.

The pear fabrics.

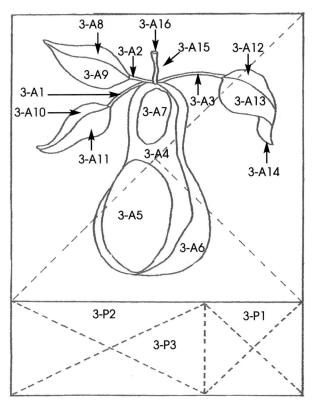

Illus. 3-1
This is the schematic of the pear. Make a copy and color it in prior to fabric selection so you have a "road map" when buying fabric.

Pear Yardage

Remember, only finished sizes are given, so add seam allowances when cutting. All measurements are figured using 44" wide fabrics and allow for seam allowances.
Background block for pear appliqué: (Yardage is given for two options, choose one.)

Option #1: Single fabric that is a 12" x 12" square.

Option #2: Pieced background block that is three triangles; 12" x 12" x 17", and two triangles each 12" x 8" x 8". These fabrics are used throughout the quilt as background blocks and the yardage is included in total yardage measurements.

Lower pieced rectangles: Cut two each from different fabrics; 3-P1, 3-P2 and 3-P3. These fabrics are used throughout the quilt as background blocks and included in the total yardage measurements.

Appliqué Fabrics:
Pear Body (3-A4): 6" x 8-1/2"
Outer body (3-A6): 4-1/2" x 8-1/2"
Upper highlight (3-A7) 2" x 3"
Lower highlight (3-A5): 3-1/2" x 5-1/2"
Leaves & stems: 12 small scraps, none larger than 3" x 4"

Definition:

Straight-of-grain refers to the fabric's weave. Threads that run the length of the fabric are the more stable, but the crosswise weave is also straight-of-grain. Pull both directions on your fabrics to see which has less give. Arrows on the templates show how to place them on fabric so it aligns on a straight-of-grain for the greatest patch stability.

Quarter-Square Triangles, the 1-1/4" Formula:

Option for piecing square 3-P1: For rotary cutting and machine piecing, there is an easy way to turn square fabric into a block of triangles. The result is straight-of-grain on all outside edges. It's easy and foolproof.

Add 1-1/4" to the desired finished square measurement. For example: the finished square measures 4" on all outside edges. Simply add 1-1/4" to 4", which equals 5-1/4". Stack two different fabrics right-sides-together (RST) and cut 5-1/4" blocks on the straight-of-grain.

Mark a diagonal line from corner to corner. A chalk marker, pencil, or permanent pen is okay for marking since this is the cutting line. Pin on both sides of the line far enough away from it so the pins stay in place during stitching. Machine stitch 1/4" away from both sides of the diagonal line. Be accurate and let the machine feed the fabric through and reduce the stitch length to 20-25 stitches per inch at the beginning and ending.

Photo 3-3
Stitch accurately 1/4" on both sides of the diagonal line.

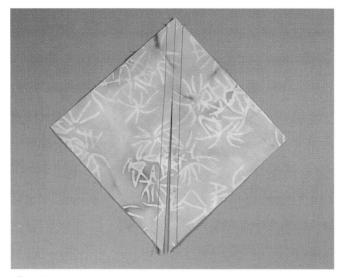

Photo 3-4
Cut the square apart on the diagonal line.

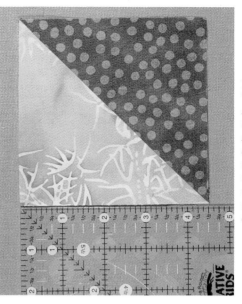

Photo 3-7
To make a half-square triangle block with straight-of-grain edges: Add 7/8" to the finished measurement and mark. Stitch, then cut apart as detailed above.

Photo 3-5
Stack two squares with the colors reversed. Match their centers, mark, and stitch as before.

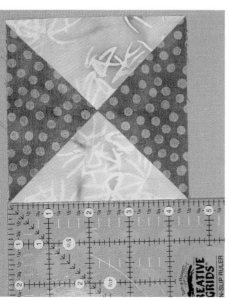

Photo 3-6
All sides of the finished quarter-square triangle block are on the straight-of-grain.

Cut apart on the marked line. Open the blocks up, and press the seam allowances to the darker fabric. Be gentle when pressing and do not stretch the fabrics.

Next, layer the two blocks together (RST), so that the colors are reversed. By touch, lock the two seam lines together at the center. Mark, pin, and stitch. Cut the blocks apart and press the seam allowances to one side.

The two finished blocks each measure 4-1/2" on all outside edges and all sides will be on the straight-of-grain. There are two of these small blocks in the quilt. Quick and easy, isn't it?

Half-square Triangles, the 7/8" Formula

Do you need half-square triangles for another project? The procedure is the same, except marking and stitching are only done once. Add 7/8" to the finished size: For a 4" square, cut two patches 4-7/8". Layer, mark, and sew on both sides of the diagonal line. Cut on the marked line and press. Two 4-1/2", half-square triangle blocks with outside edges on the straight-of-grain are completed.

Hand Piecing

This is a brief overview of hand piecing (see Introduction, Piecing Basics, page 13), no matter the size of the patches or blocks. Cut a template from a sturdy material; Mylar™ works well. Trace the pattern on the matte side, being sure to include the patch numbers, how many to cut, and the straight-of-grain line. *Do not* include seam allowances in the template. Lay the template on the *wrong side* of the fabric and trace around it with a mechanical pencil. This is your stitching line. Each patch is marked separately. Repeat for the number needed, leaving 1/2" between the pencil lines. Cut out the patches in between the pencil lines and the seam allowance is automatically included. Many same-sized patches can be strung together on a knotted thread; if the stack gets knocked over, the patches stay together. Do this for appliqué patches also.

Constructing the Pear Block

Piece the background block or use a single fabric. Transfer the Master Pattern to it or use one of the other options detailed in Chapter 1. Cut out the appliqué patches and leave the paper patterns pinned on until ready to appliqué.

Piecing the Lower Blocks

Assembly of the rectangular pieced blocks is easy. Either by machine or hand, the block is joined as in Illus. 3-2, one 3-P2 to a 3-P3 with a straight seam. Repeat for the block's remaining half and join the two halves together, making sure that the center is matched accurately. Pin and stitch. Piece the two blocks together, but don't join it to the pear block until the appliqué is completed.

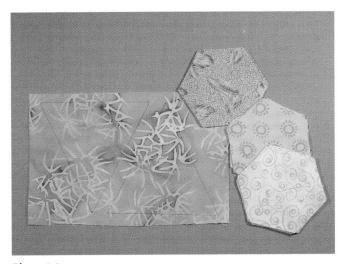

Photo 3-8
Patches cut out and strung together for later use.

For machine sewing, match the center in the same manner as when sewing the quarter-square triangles (see photo 3-5). For hand piecing, accuracy is equally important, but the finished size template lines must be marked as discussed in the beginning of this chapter. Once marked, the width of the seam line is not crucial. The pencil marks are important because they are the stitching lines and exact pinning is required on both patches. Notice that the cut edges in the example may not be even—and it does not matter in hand piecing. The line is what is significant. However, it is critical in machine piecing, as the seam allowances' cut edges are matched for stitching.

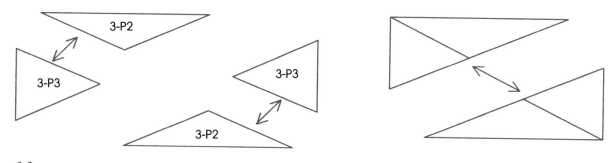

Illus. 3-2
Here you see the assembly sequence of pieced blocks. All rectangular blocks in the book are pieced in the same manner, whether by hand or machine.

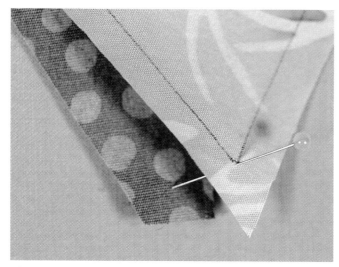

Photo 3-9
With RST, pin into the exact corners of the pencil line.

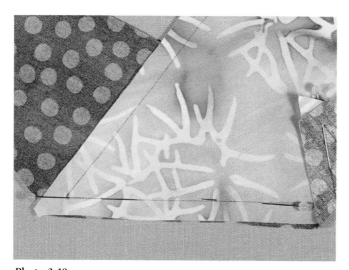

Photo 3-10
Pin on the interior pencil lines of both patches and the remaining corner.

Place the patches RST along the pencil lines that need to be sewn together. Are you confused as to which edges go together? Lay the entire block out, right side up. Flip one patch over RST on the patch to be joined. I always do this to prevent sewing wrong sides together. To begin, pin one end of the seam line by stabbing a pin into the exact corner of *both patches*. Angle the pin inward.

If the seam is long, use enough pins to align the stitching line, always pinning on the pencil lines of both patches. Then pin the remaining corner.

Thread the needle and knot the end where it was cut from the spool. Refer to Chapter 1: Quilting Basics (page 10) for more detailed information. A right-handed stitcher will sew right to left, while a left-handed person will sew left to right. Hold the two patches securely between thumb and forefinger, and remove the first pin. Put the needle into the corner exactly where the pinholes are on *both* fabric patches.

Take a tiny stitch, about 1/8" long. Pull the thread through, and backstitch halfway to the knot then bring the needle forward about 1/8". Be sure the needle is on *both* pencil lines. This backstitch is used when beginning or ending any seams to provide extra security at the ends.

Photo 3-11
Remove the corner pin and poke the needle into the hole left by the pin on both patches.

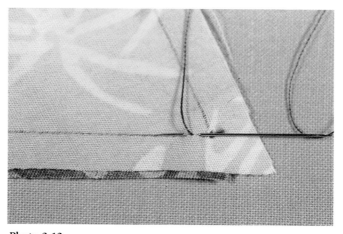

Photo 3-12
Take a tiny backstitch at the beginning of the pencil line and backstitch when ending the seam. The thread must be on the pencil lines of both fabrics.

Stitch along the pencil lines of both patches, removing pins as needed. Even an expert hand piecer must constantly look on the under patch to ensure that the stitching is on the lower patch's pencil line. If off, remove the needle, adjust the patches, and continue stitching. Pull the thread through after four or five stitches are on the needle. If the fabric seems puckered, gently pull the stitched area between thumb and finger to remove the gathered fabric. Do not apply excess pressure on the fabric. It could stretch. Repeat for the remaining two patches. If ragged seam allowances bother you, now is the time to trim them.

Stitch Length

Needle size (finer needles make smaller stitches), practice, density of fabric weaves, and finger dexterity determine stitch length. A quilter who has arthritis cannot make as small a stitch as someone without finger problems, but that may apply to age. Do not make stitches longer than 1/4". Smaller is always better. It is much easier to take small stitches, about 1/16", if the fabric is moved up and down onto the needle's tip, rather than moving the needle. This may feel awkward at first, but it does produce smaller stitches and is much faster. Pull gently on the seam line of two patches to see how stitch size affects it. Threads are visible and the seam pulls apart with longer stitches.

Congratulations! If this is your first experience with hand piecing, you have just learned the basic elements. In any block, there can be more patches, shapes, or sizes, but sewing any straight seam is the same.

Joining the two halves together requires pin matching. It's easy. With double patches RST, pin through the thread holes of the two opposing patches. One pin is sufficient.

Photo 3-13
Pick up four to five stitches and pull the needle through. The stitches on the right are smooth. The ones to the left are puckered. Pull the fabric gently between thumb and finger at the stitching line to remove the slight gathering.

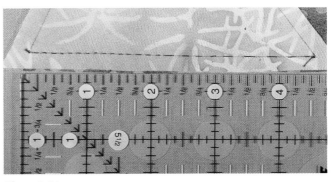

Photo 3-14
Larger stitches on the right allow the seams to gap. Try to reduce stitch length.

Photo 3-15
At a center, pin directly into the last thread hole of one patch directly across to the thread hole of the joining patch.

Important Information:
Never stitch into the seam allowance when hand piecing and most machine piecing. Doing so nails the seam in place and creates seam lumps when pressing. Sewing through seam lines is acceptable only when machine piecing long strips together, as in the border, and when constructing the two brick blocks in Chapter 5.

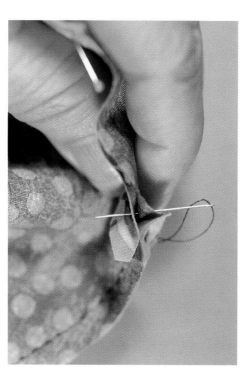

Photo 3-16
When sewing, stab the needle through the seam allowance at the stitch line. Never sew into a seam allowance.

Photo 3-17
The intersection of any points should meet perfectly.

Pin the remaining seam line and sew as before until reaching the center. Run the needle from one patch to the other at the *stitching line*. Pull the thread through on the under patch. Poke the needle back up to the top patch, taking a regular stitch length.

Take a backstitch right into the center and continue sewing to the end. Knot and cut the thread. Press the seams toward the larger triangle—in this instance, to the turquoise dot fabric. Be careful; do not pull on the block when pressing. The four seams should meet exactly in the center. All piecing for the remainder of the **Savory Garden** blocks is done in the same manner.

Appliquéing the Pear

The background block is ready to appliqué. The examples use the Master Pattern technique. Refer to the Introduction, Master Pattern, and Chapter 1, for a summary. Cut out all appliqué patches adding 1/4" seam allowances on all sides. The patches that are farthest away go on first (see Chapter 2, Appliqué Fundamentals, page 29), in this case, the leaf stems. The flower has broad stems, and each side was turned under and appliquéd in place, but that will not work for narrow stems that require tiny seam allowances.

Narrow Stems

It is not necessary to cut a template pattern since these three stems are so narrow and have gentle curves. Simply cut bias strips 1/2" wide and 1/2" longer than each stem.

Lay the stem patch wrong side up over the inside (smaller arc) curve. This edge is always sewn first. The fabric will curve away from the pencil stitching line and may look as if it will not fit in place, especially if the stem has a severe arc.

Definition:

A bias strip is a piece of fabric cut off-grain. True bias is cut at a 45 degree angle to the fabric's straight-of-grain weave. In practice, anything cut off grain can be manipulated around a curve or arc so it will lay flat when stitched in place.

Begin the running stitch in the end seam allowance. Use the needle's tip to move the fabric into place, taking only two or three stitches at a time. The stitches must be tiny or this method will look sloppy. Don't worry about the excess, wavy seam allowance.

The running stitch should be on the pencil line. However, the line is covered by fabric. To see it, fold the stem fabric back on itself and check that the needle is on the line. Verify that the needle is on the pencil line each time before pulling the needle through.

Continue moving the fabric into place and stitch down the entire side, ending in the seam allowance. Knot and cut the thread. The seam allowance must be trimmed so that it is within the two pencil lines. Using small scissors, carefully trim away the excess. It is possible to trim the seam allowance down to 1/16". Next, roll the stem right side up into place. Trim the remaining seam allowance as you appliqué to the end. The seam allowance will be very narrow, but it is possible to needleturn it under.

If necessary, trim away any excess seam allowance in the stem ends. The stem is complete. Repeat for the remaining stems. Last is the pear's stem. Refer to the next chapter (Flowers Times Three) directions for appliquéing the pear stem's top (see Ovals and Circles, page 51).

Points

There are two types of points. Leaf 3-A10 and 11 are the easiest. Begin appliquéing the 3-A10 patch at its top center, not the stem end. Stitch toward the point and take a stitch exactly into the fabric at the pencil point. The seam allowance will be very narrow.

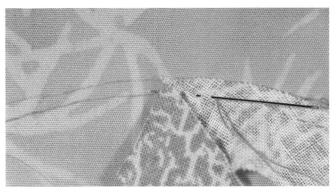

Photo 3-19
With the needle in the fabric, fold the bias strip back and check to see the needle is on the pencil line. If not, remove the needle, reposition the fabric, and try again.

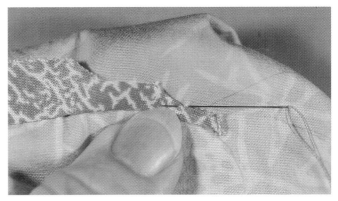

Photo 3-20
Trim the seam allowance as you stitch. It will be very narrow.

Photo 3-21
The completed stem is 1/8" wide.

Photo 3-18
Lay a narrow bias strip over the bottom stem line and sew with a small running stitch.

Photo 3-22
Stitch toward the leaf's point. The seam allowance will be narrow; tightly woven fabric is an advantage.

Photo 3-23
Flat fold the seam allowance under. This is not a sharp point.

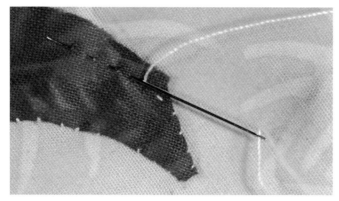

Photo 3-24
Stitch across the end and down the side, then baste the remaining edge that will be covered by the lower patch.

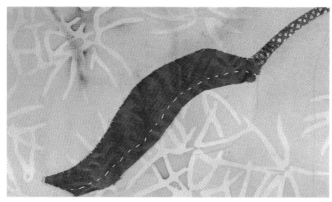

Photo 3-25
At the stem end, begin the appliqué stitch again. Continue trimming and folding under the seam allowance until the sewing is completed.

Photo 3-26
The contrasting thread shows how the lower leaf was sewn.

Now, push the fabric under using the point of the needle. Too much fussing and the fabric will fray. The seam allowance is just folded under, rather similar to a flat fold, because the lower leaf will cover most of the seam allowance.

Sew a running stitch inside the seam allowance to attach the loose bottom edge that will be covered by 3-A11. Finish appliquéing back to the starting point. Trim the seam.

Patch 3-A11 is sewn next, starting in the center of its bottom edge. Stitch toward the stem. Left-handers start on the top edge and sew toward the stem. But how do you know where to sew because the vein's center line is covered by the 3-A10? It's easy. Lay the template pattern for 3-A10 in position and pencil mark the center vein.

Stitch patch 3-A11 up to the stem and flat fold the end under and continue appliquéing on the vein line to the point. Take a stitch right into the point. Trim the folded-under seam allowance to 1/16". Push the point back into its seam allowance, not between the seam allowance, and the upper leaf or background block. This may seem unnecessary, but it makes the point less thick.

Take another stitch right into the point to nail it in place. Use the side of the needle and push the fabric under. Trim the seam allowance if necessary. Stitch close together until the point is secure. Stitch to the end, knot, and cut the thread. Finish the leaves and appliqué the pear's body.

HINTS:

❖ Never start sewing at the height or depth of a curve.

❖ The tighter the curves, the narrower the seam allowances.

❖ Never start or end stitching at a point.

❖ Clip into concave (inside) curves to relax the seam allowance.

Pattern Layering

On patch 3-A11, you retraced the missing stitching line for the vein. I call this technique pattern layering. Layering one fabric on top of another is common in appliqué. But once the bottom fabric is attached, any pattern lines for top patches get covered up, no matter what sewing method is used. To reestablish the appliqué locations, position the template in its proper location and trace the missing line(s). For the pear, this is done for all the leaves. In the pear's body, patches 3-A5, 3-A6 and 3-A7 must all have their lines marked on top of 3-A4. This simple technique is used in most of the Savory Garden's blocks.

ADDITIONAL THOUGHTS:

Are you having trouble controlling the patches or appliqué? Perhaps you are holding it in the air and the fabric is flopping about. Place the work in your lap and rest the heel of the hand that holds the needle on your leg for stability. This method controls the fabric and helps equalize thread tension when pulling the thread through the fabric.

In succeeding chapters, there is more information about other options and less on needle-turn appliqué. Remember, you can mix-and-match techniques. Perhaps appliquéing a stem with the methods just detailed makes sense because of its narrow width, but you want to buttonhole the leaf or use another method in the remainder of the block. This is your quilt: The decision is yours, and "option" is the name of the game.

chapter 4

Three Flowers Times Two

Photo 4-1
The stemmed flowers.

This chapter details buttonhole stitching on the three blossoms. It also expands needleturn appliqué techniques with a unique method to fold fabric over and encase petal interiors. We will explore, using the wrong side of the fabric, how to appliqué acute curves and make effortless oval and circular flower centers. Also covered are machine options for embroidery.

The Stemmed Flowers

Three Flowers Yardage:
Background block: 12" x 16"
Appliqué fabrics:
  Stems: 8" x 13"
  Flower centers: 6" x 6"
  Petals: 8" x 8" of main color, 6" x 6" of contrast. Flowers can be different colors.

Three Blossoms

Three Blossoms Yardage
Background block: 4" x 16"
Flowers: Three fabrics, each 4" x 4"
Flower centers: 2" x 2"
Triangles: 4-P1, 4-P2R, cut two, each 2" x 2" x 2-7/8" for the quilt block. One template must be turned over for the reverse.

4-P2, cut 1, 3-1/2" x 16-1/2"
4-P3, cut 1, 4-1/2" x 10-1/2"
4-P4, 4-1/2" x 9"

Pillow Yardage (1/2" seams included in measurements)
Background block: 6" x 17"
Triangles: 4-P1, 4-P1R, cut two, each 2-1/2" x 3-1/2", one is reversed
Side rectangles: Cut two 5-1/2" x 17"
Cording: 3 yards (approximate only)
Pillow backing: 17" x 17"
Pillow insert: 16" x 16"

Photo 4-2
Three blossoms. The bottom triangles are pieced onto the block after the appliqué is completed. The outer block on the right is pieced and joined to it.

Photo 4-3
The fabrics.

The stems are appliquéd on first, the petals are next and, finally, the flower center covers all of the petal's seam allowance raw ends. The tiny pieces may look difficult, but the seam allowances extend under the flower's center. You always have the option of enlarging any shape to create more gentle curves or relaxed points.

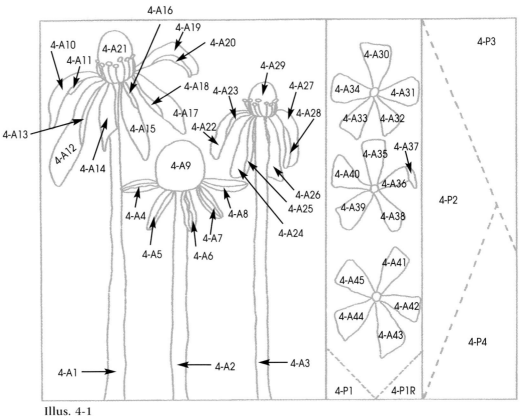

Illus. 4-1
The schematics for the stemmed flowers, three blossoms, and pieced block.

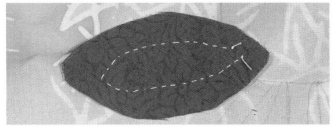

Photo 4-4
Cut the petal shape 1/2" larger than the template and sew it in place, wrong side up, with a running stitch.

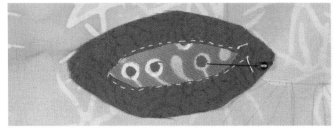

Photo 4-5
Cut the petal's interior smaller than the running stitch shape and pin it in place.

Photo 4-6
Push the fabric into position and appliqué the edge, working in the excess.

Photo 4-7
About 1/2" before the point, fold the fabric tip over and pin it in place.

Photo 4-8
Working up the remaining side, fold the fabric in and appliqué.

Photo 4-9
The completed petal. Stitching is close together to control the excess fabric.

Encasing Petal Interiors

These patches are cut out so the wrong side of the fabric faces up; select, therefore, a fabric that is attractive on both sides. A running stitch attaches this patch. The petal's interior is laid in place and the main fabric is folded over and stitched down. This unusual method of appliqué is also used for the pea pods.

To begin, cut the patch *on the bias,* and large enough to include the fold-over—1/2" larger on both long edges. In this instance, bigger is better; the excess can be trimmed away. Pin the patch over the petal's location. Using a matching thread, attach it with a running stitch that follows the petals outer edges. Refer to Chapter 3, Narrow stems (page 42).

Cut the interior fabric smaller than the running stitching shape. Pin it in place.

A pencil line can be drawn on the interior so that you can appliqué to a line, but I simply fold it over and stitch. After all, these are flowers and no two are alike. Begin appliqué by rolling over the outer fabric and turning under a narrow seam allowance. Push the fabric straight up with your fingernail to just cover the running stitch. The seam allowance will pucker and needs to be trimmed. However, do not trim too close or push the fabric forward at an angle. The flower's inner edge will be ruffled. Use this excess fabric to create an irregular line.

About 1/2" before reaching the petal's point, trim it to about 1/8" and fold the fabric toward the center. Pin it in place.

Continue folding the seam allowance in and stitch it down to the point.

Trim the upper seam allowance at this point. Fold and tuck it under. The fabric will angle up and have a blunt point. Take several stitches. Continue trimming and sewing back to the flower's center.

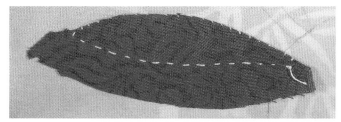

Photo 4-10
Place the fabric wrong side up and appliqué one edge, stopping two stitches before the point. With the same thread, sew a running stitch down the remaining side.

An adaptation is used on two other petals (4-A5 and 4-A8). One side is appliquéd in the traditional manner and the other seam allowance is rolled over. Begin with the fabric wrong side up and appliqué the first edge, stopping about two stitches before the point. Continue with a running stitch over the pencil line back to the beginning. One edge is now appliquéd in position and the other is attached with a running stitch.

With a new thread, bring the needle up from the background block. Trim the point's top edge, fold it over and push it under.

Take a stitch, while tucking in any loose threads from the free edge—there will be several. Do not worry, taking stitches close together seals the raw edges.

Continue to trim, fold, and stitch in the traditional needleturn technique back to the starting point. You will be sewing toward your body. The seam allowance is wavy. Use it to create an uneven edge.

Other Options

There are other options if this technique is not for you. The petal can be appliquéd in two sections. Place the lower petal fabric wrong side up, and appliqué then layer and appliqué the upper fabric over it—or, machine appliqué each section with a satin stitch, using a stabilizing product under the background block to prevent rippling (see Chapter 6).

Stamens and Remaining Petals

The other petals are regular appliqué. If you encounter trouble with long, narrow points, change their shapes to more gentle curves. Stamens can be hand or machine embroidered and stitched in a thread of your choice.

Photo 4-11
With a new thread, fold the fabric point over the appliqué.

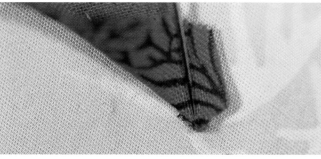

Photo 4-12
Trim close and push the fabric under with the side of the needle.

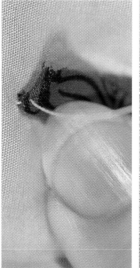 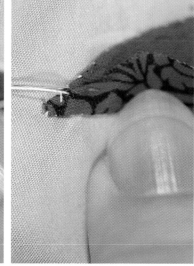

Photo 4-13
Take a stitch right in the point.

Photo 4-14
Continue stitching close together and trim as necessary.

Photo 4-15
The completed petal.

Tight Convex Curves

There is nothing different about appliquéing a curve except that the seam allowance must be narrow and trimmed about a scant 1/2" ahead of the stitching. If you trim too far ahead of the thread, you may have to start over because the piece has shifted. Glue-basting will help prevent this, but place the glue dots at least 1/2" away from the edge.

Shifting Appliqué Patches

What if patches shift or the fabric ripples? The fingers under the background block pulling the fabric backward while the thumb is pushing the patch forward cause this. Be aware of how you hold the fabric and the pressure your fingers exert. Apply equal, directly-opposing finger pressure, and *do not* hold the fabric in a "death grip." Hold it delicately between thumb and middle finger. It helps to roll the excess background block rather than wadding it in your hand. This also prevents wrinkling.

Three Blossoms: A Quilt Block and a Pillow

The techniques for needleturn appliqué have already been covered to create this design. This section deals will the buttonhole stitch, thread types, and the flowers' centers—oval and round. Refer to Chapter 1: Buttonhole Stitch (page 19) for details. In addition to the quilt block, the design is also perfect for a pillow.

Buttonhole Stitch and Using a Hoop

Is an embroidery hoop necessary to hold the fabric while stitching? If you are more comfortable using one, do so. I did not. If the stitches are puckering the background, however, a hoop is necessary. Do remove a hoop each time you stop stitching to prevent permanent marks forming in the fabric.

Easy and fast, the buttonhole stitch is very decorative. Once the patch is prepared for attaching to the background block the (raw edge, basted edge or fused), it is ready for stitching. There are a number of thread options that are dictated by personal preference. Perle cotton #8 has a high sheen and is easy to use. Embroidery floss (no more than three strands)

has a matte look and comes in a wide selection of colors. Metallics and novelty threads work well with a sewing machine. The example is linen thread, which is uneven in thickness. There is no one best thread choice, and types and colors could be changed for each flower. Stitch samples to see which you prefer.

Use a thread length no more than 18" with a single knot and an embroidery needle large enough to accommodate the thread. To begin, hold the fabric so you will be stitching toward yourself, with the patch's end seam allowance to the left (reverse for left-handers). Bring the needle up from the background block and into the patch as deep as you want the stitches to be long. The sample stitches are 1/8" and the sample has the raw edges basted under.

Take the needle into the patch and through the background block. Bring the needle up just past the edge of the patch and loop the thread around the needle's tip.

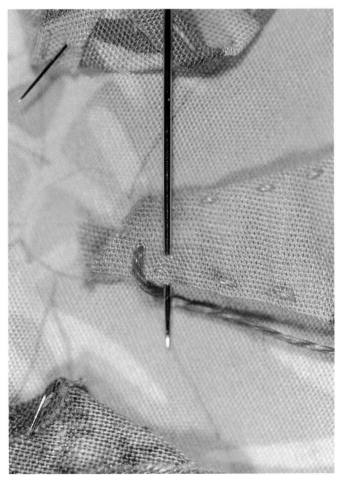

Photo 4-16
Bring the needle up just past the edge of the patch.

Pull the needle through. Thread tension is important. Pulling it too tight makes the fabric bunch under the stitch, but too loose will allow fabric movement. Take the next stitch, loop the thread as before, and pull the needle through. Be sure that the stitch depth and spaces are consistent.

Turning corners or points is not difficult. It requires three stitches all using the same thread hole. The first stitch goes slightly to the right of the corner or point, the next is in the exact center, and the final stitch is slightly to the right.

To end the thread, take the needle to the back of the work right after the thread has looped around the needle and been pulled tight. Yes, it can be knotted, but I prefer working the thread through the stitching and back again, piercing the strand when the thread is woven back upon itself. This is a technique used in embroidery work, where there should be no knots. It can also be used at the thread's beginning by leaving a tail long enough to weave in once the stitching is completed.

Ovals and Circles

Large ovals and rounds over 1" in diameter are appliquéd to a pencil line using a narrow 1/16" seam allowance. When the shapes are smaller, it is better to use a different technique.

Cut an oval or circle 1/4" to 1/2" larger than the finished size, in this instance, 3/4" x 1". It might take one or two tries until the exact size of the cut shape is determined. Knot a single thread and take tiny, even stitches 1/16" in from the edge of the oval or circle working from the right side of the fabric. The stitches and spaces should be the same length to have the fabric gather evenly. Do not cut the thread. Gather the fabric, but be careful to pull in the same direction you sewed. Otherwise, the tiny seam allowance can fray. It helps to stick your finger in the center when pulling. Gather until tight. The oval will look uneven and be lumpy. Using the tip of the needle, pull the edges and shape it into an oval. It is ready to be stitched to the flower's center area with the gathering thread. Take stitches that are close together. If a point forms that is difficult to remove, take a stitch right into the point and

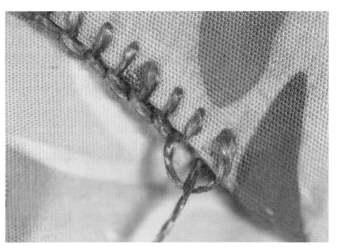

Photo 4-17
Tension is important when the thread is pulled snug. Too much tension, and the fabric puckers; too loose and the fabric ravels or shifts.

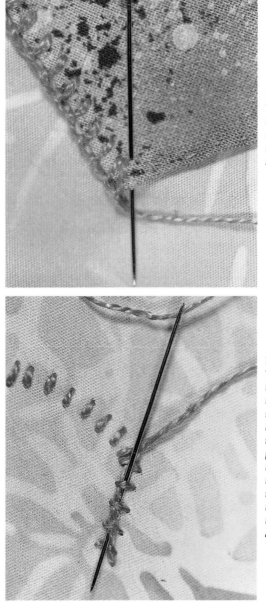

Photo 4-18
Take two or three stitches in the corner, using the same hole.

Photo 4-19
To end the thread, run the needle under the loops on the wrong side, pull the thread through, reverse direction, pierce the thread, and cut.

Photo 4-20
Cut an oval and sew an even running stitch close to the edge. Gather the fabric and stitch it with the same thread.

Photo 4-21
Make an exact circle by placing a washer in the center and gathering. Douse with spray starch, and iron dry. Remove the washer, re-gather, and sew in place.

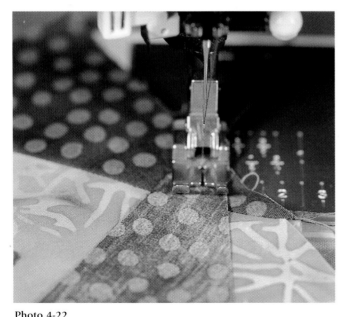

Photo 4-22
Stitch the small triangles to the bottom of the three blossoms with a 1/4" seam.

pull. It will disappear. Just before completing the appliqué is the time to add stuffing if you want more loft than the seam allowance creates. Do not over stuff. It distorts the background fabric.

Perfect Circles

It is easy to make a perfect circle. Use the same method as for ovals up to the gathering. Before gathering, slip a metal washer into the center and gather it. Lay the piece on an ironing board and, with the gathers wrong side up, douse it with spray starch. Iron it dry—carefully, the washers get hot! When the fabric has dried completely, open up the gathers and remove the washer. Easy does it—the narrow seam allowances can fray. Re-gather the fabric into a perfect circle and stitch it onto your design using the gathering thread.

Machine Piecing the Triangles

Caution: Add 1/4" seam allowances to every patch when machine piecing, and cut so the outer edges are on straight-of-grain. Refer to Chapter 2, page 32, for additional information.

Cut the two bottom triangles, 4-P1 4-P1R (reversed). They are *not* equal triangles and the template must be flipped over before cutting. Stitch to the bottom of the Three Blossoms. It might be easier to have the diagonal pencil line on the fabric, as in hand piecing, so that the triangles are aligned properly. Stitch using 20-25 stitches per inch. Flip the triangle right side up and press. Repeat for the second triangle. Stitch the outer edges in place within the seam allowance. Press.

The large block to the right of three blossoms can be machine pieced. The block is assembled in the same manner as detailed in Chapter 2. This triangle is repeated throughout the quilt, varying only in fabrics and template size. First, join 4-P2 to 4-P4. Press the seam toward the larger triangle. Add 4-P3 to the diagonal edge. Press the seam toward the center of the block. This block is joined to the side of three blossoms. Refer to Illus. 4-1, page 47, for placement.

Pillow Construction

Note: The flower centers may have to be enlarged to cover the excess bulk created by the buttonhole stitching.

Cut the background block 7" x 17" (1/2" seam allowances are included).

To the side and bottom edges of the pattern, make *1/2" seams*. The diagonal line has a 1/4" seam for machine piecing accuracy. These triangles are not equal, so they must be cut separately facing two directions, or cut both at once with wrong sides of the fabric together. Stitch the triangles 4-P1 and 4-P1R onto the bottom of the three blossoms.

Once the design is completed, press it from the wrong side to keep the dimensional appearance. Back the rectangle with a neutral colored fabric to provide extra body. Sew cording or trim around the block. Push a thick ruler against the cording to prevent shifting during stitching.

Photo 4-23
Hold a thick ruler against cording and push in when stitching. This keeps the stitching tight against the cording.

Add the side panels and any trim desired to the outside edges. Stitch the backing to the pillow top, leaving an opening to turn it right side out. Turn and insert a pillow form.

The finished pillow.

ADDITIONAL THOUGHTS

Always measure each completed block against finished measurements. Is it accurate? Rejoice if it is—your techniques are exceptional. If the block falls short of the correct measurements or is too big, this is the time to figure out where the error(s) occurred. Perhaps your 1/4" foot or guide on the sewing machine does not correspond to the ruler. Next, check the templates against the book's patterns. Now, check your sewing machine technique. A wavy stitching line results in uneven seams that don't fit together. Learn to guide the fabric in a straight line under the presser foot. Even tiny discrepancies will multiply when added to other errors and cause major assembly problems.

Am I putting too much emphasis on accuracy? No. I admit I am a stickler about points meeting, intersecting seams that actually intersect and square quilts. It does take longer to produce a quilt that is accurate. Your frustration level will be dramatically reduced when everything goes together without trying to force to match seams that are different lengths. Practice accuracy and enjoy the process. It really is less work and the results are worth the few extra minutes it takes to be precise.

But is my level of precision the same as yours? Emphatically not! Everyone has different expectations and degrees of hand dexterity. Strive to find and reach your own level. Rather than thinking of all the unfamiliar techniques to be learned, approach the quilt bit by bit. Work on one technique and perfect it to your own capabilities, then move on the to next. With time and practice, your work will improve, no matter your level of expertise. Non-quilters frequently say that that it takes a lot of patience to be a quilter. Not in my case. I have very little patience, but I do persevere.

chapter 5

Bricks, Snail, Leaf, and Moss

Bricks are easy to machine piece, and function as a foil for the leaf, moss, and snail appliqués. They can be rearranged into a pattern of your choice. If you choose to piece the bricks in a fancier design, the background should not overwhelm the appliquéd shapes or they could disappear visually. Another arrangement, with more muted brick colors than the ones in the sample, will allow the appliqué to pop forward.

Photo 5-1
The snail block.

Photo 5-3
The snail fabrics.

Photo 5-2
The leaf block.

Photo 5-4
The leaf fabrics.

THE BRICKS AND APPLIQUÉ DESIGNS

Yardage: Each brick is 2" x 3-1/2"; approximately 41 are needed per single block. Yardage amount depends on the number of fabrics chosen, but 1/4 yd of four or five fabrics is ample for two blocks. If the outer borders are made from the same brick colors, 3/4 to 1 yd of three to five fabrics is sufficient for all the bricks.

Snail under shell and spiral: 5" x 5", cut two of contrasting fabrics

Snail head and tail: 5" x 5"

Leaf: 8" x 7"

Moss: 8" x 8"

can work, but keep in mind that the appliqués will be lost against too busy a background. To compensate for this, select bolder appliqué colors. Since the bricks also form the quilt's borders, the colors and print designs must complement all of the block fabrics and colors.

Cutting the Bricks

Each cut brick measures 2-1/2" x 4". Finished size is 2" x 3-1/2". A rotary cutter is perfect for cutting multiples and machine piecing. Fold each fabric with selvedges together. Stack three fabrics (six layers) with the selvedge edges meeting. Cut across one 22" end from the centerfold to selvedge to establish the straight-of-grain line. Next, cut the fabrics into 2-1/2" wide strips. Cut the strips into 4" long bricks. All sides are on the straight-of-grain to eliminate stretching. For hand piecing, make a template the finished size. Trace around the template for the stitching line and cut adding a 1/4" seam allowance.

Choosing Brick Fabrics

Batik fabrics with plenty of color and pattern are especially good for the bricks and only three fabrics are necessary, but enough color variation provides movement and interest. What if you choose homespun fabrics, plaids, or 1930s reproduction fabrics? Batiks will clash. In those instances, five, six, or even seven fabrics

Hint

Is choosing brick fabrics driving you crazy? Wait to select the fabrics until several blocks are completed and take them to the store for evaluation or cut a variety of fabrics into bricks and move them around until the colors and prints are pleasing. It took me several tries before I made my selections. No one brick should say, "Hey, look at me! Aren't I a grand choice?" They should blend together as a whole unit rather than look like a grouping of individual bricks that have no color relationship. Refer back to the Introduction: Additional Thoughts, for a color selection discussion.

Piecing the Bricks

The bricks are laid out differently in the two examples (see Photos 5-1 and 5-2). The snail block has no brick border, while the leaf block does. The bricks can be the same or different. Whatever your decision, lay them out on a table and position the colors to your liking. This allows the bricks to be arranged so that no two fabrics blend into each other and look like a double brick. Partial bricks will be needed on some rows. Refer to Illus. 5-1. Once the layout is finalized, stitching is next.

Pin each row of bricks end-to-end and machine stitch together. Sew from cut edge to cut edge. If hand piecing, do not sew into the seam allowance. Press the seam allowances of each row in the same direction. No seams intersect so there is no bulk when joining the rows together. Refer to the Introduction (Piecing Basics) for an overview. Press the block. It is now ready for appliqué.

Photo 5-5
The bricks are sewn together to the raw edges.

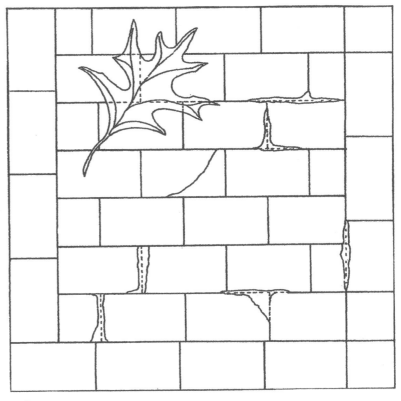

Illus. 5-1
The bricks schematics with the snail and leaf.

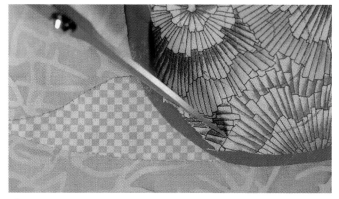

Photo 5-6
Begin cutting the spiral midway between the lines *at the bottom opening.*

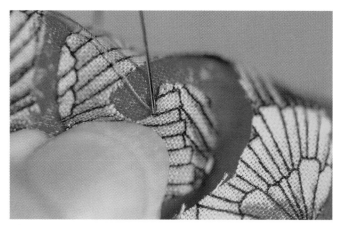

Photo 5-7
Tuck the center under and stitch close together to hold the narrow seam allowance.

THE APPLIQUE DESIGNS

The Snail—Needleturn

Using your favorite method, transfer the snail shape to the brick block, but do not transfer the spiral shell design. Two fabrics of the same size are required for the snail shell: The under shell (add seam allowances) and the spiral, cut the exact size of the template. To both, add the tail and head locations on the wrong side. This is necessary to get the spiral in the correct placement. Transfer the spiral design to the spiral fabric's right side.

Once the appliqué design is ready, cut the fabrics and begin appliqué. Options for the feelers are machine satin stitch, narrow ribbon, embroidery, and fabric (as in the sample).

Appliqué, machine, or ribbon work is done first, but embroidery is stitched after the head appliqué is completed. The eyes can be French knots.

For both needleturn appliqué and machine, stitch the head, tail, and then the under shell. No spiral lines are placed on the under shell. Needleturn the under shell the same way as explained for the flower centers of the Three Tall Flowers pattern in the preceding chapter. Trim seam allowances to a scant 1/2". The stitches are close together and about 1/16" apart.

Next, lay the uncut spiral fabric with the spiral traced on the right side of the fabric over the under shell and match the marks for tail and head and pin in place. Glue-basting can be used, but I find that two pins do the job. Do not cut the spiral. The spiral's outer edge is appliquéd first with a narrow seam allowance. Begin sewing about 1-1/2" up from where the spiral starts on the bottom outer edge. Fold under enough of the spiral's seam allowance so that 1/4" of the under shell is exposed. This is not an exact measurement and is more interesting if it is not even. Stitch around the entire spiral shell until approaching the beginning where the spiral marking starts. The beginning of the spiral is very pointed. Do not panic, later this is trimmed to a manageable angle for turning.

Cut the fabric midway between the spiral lines as stitching proceeds into its center. The inside curve will have seam allowances no wider than 1/2" (see Photo 5-8). To turn the center, place the needle a scant 1/4" ahead of the inside cut and sweep it back to the center. Stitches should be very close together to prevent raveling the narrow seam allowance.

Hint

Have you wondered if you can appliqué through layers of fabric into the background block? The answer is yes, unless there is a design reason to have the top layer appear as if it is floating over the lower layer. For the spiral, all edges should be stitched through to the background block.

Continue sweeping and stitching by placing the needle under the seam allowance and pulling back toward the stitched area so that the seam allowance rolls under. The fabric will roll under like a dream if it is clipped two or three threads deep every 1/4" or so. As the curve gets bigger, you can roll farther out from the stitching as much as an inch.

When close to the end, trim about 1/2" off the long tail. Trim the seam allowance on the stitched side to about 1/16".

Fold under the point into the seam allowance by hand and trim.

Flip the fabric right side up, trim as necessary, and complete stitching the point.

Photo 5-8
Continue to sweep the needle and roll the fabric under, working toward the outside.

Photo 5-10
Trim the both sides of the seam allowance as stitching progresses. Too much and the seams cannot be rolled under.

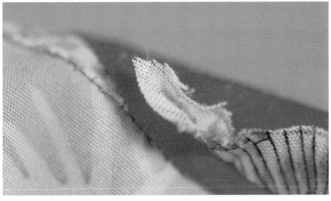

Photo 5-9
The tail, ready for trimming, is loose on both sides.

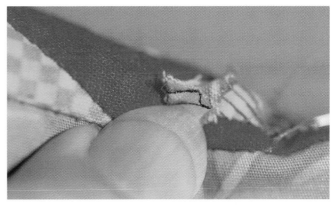

Photo 5-11
Fold back the point's seam allowance and appliqué the seam.

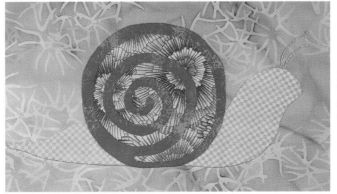

Photo 5-12
The completed needleturn appliqué snail.

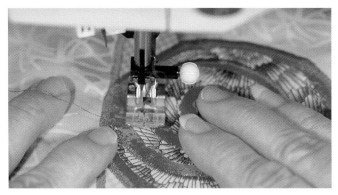

Photo 5-13
The straight stitch holds the patch edges in place so they do not ripple when satin stitched.

Photo 5-15
The back of the snail shows excess Wash-A-Way Paper being removed.

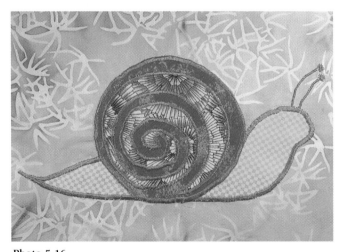

Photo 5-16
The complete machine satin stitched snail.

The Snail—Machine Appliqué

For machine appliqué, it is essential to use a stabilizer to prevent warping the fabric, especially wavy lines that occur around curves or circles. A hoop to keep the fabric stretched may be necessary. However, using a paper wash-a-way stabilizer means that you do not need a hoop. Every machine handles fabric differently and a test sample is mandatory. Once the stabilizer and hoop or-not-to-hoop decisions are made, cut out the patches, leaving seam allowances on the head and tail only where the shell will cover them. Glue-baste the head and tail in position, making sure that the glue dots are in the patch interiors. Straight stitch the head and tail with the decorative thread.

It is time for the decorative stitching. The sample is stitched 4mm wide with high luster rayon thread. Stitch the eyes first, then the antenna. Next, satin stitch around the head, except on the end where it will be covered by the shell. If you use something other than a satin stitch, make sure that it covers the fabric edges to prevent fraying.

Cut the spiral on the pencil lines. Remember, with machine stitching, there is no seam allowance, so it has to be removed before sewing begins. Position the spiral on the under shell and glue-baste or pin in position. Begin straight stitching at the spiral's opening. Stitch up to the center and return to the bottom.

It is ready for a satin or another decorative stitch. Even with the edges straight stitched, they may creep. For control, hold the fabric with a seam ripper as it goes under the presser foot. See Photo 5-13. Refer to the directions for reducing and increasing the satin stitch on the tail and stitch the spiral's point in the same manner.

The sample used wash-a-way paper that easily tears away once it is satin stitched. The excess was removed and the block was dunked in water to dissolve the paper under the stitching.

❖ *If the machine has a needle-down position, use it. When stitching around a curve, stop the needle in the fabric on the outside of the zigzag, lift the presser foot and rotate the fabric enough to stitch a slight arc. Stitch a short distance and repeat the procedure until the curve is completed.*

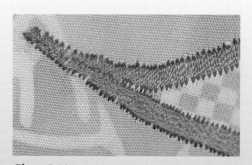

Photo 5-14
A graduated satin stitch is used to create a pointed tail.

❖ *Stitching the tail is not difficult, but the tip needs to be sewn slowly for this method to be reduced properly. About 1/2" before the point, stop the machine and, with the needle down, decrease the zigzag width from 4mm to 3.5mm. Resume sewing for 1/2". Stop and reduce the zigzag to 3mm. Continue reducing in this manner to the point until the width is 2mm. Stitch off the tail for about 1/2"; stop and rotate the fabric to stitch the remaining side of the tail, increasing the zigzag width in the same manner it was narrowed.*

The Leaf and Moss Appliqué

The leaf and moss appliqué are not different from the snail, only the shapes and sizes change, and there are numerous points in the leaf. In the **What a Garden!** quilt, the leaf is needleturn appliquéd. Refer to Chapter 3, Points, and photos 3-22 to 3-24 (page 43). Another option is to use metallic threads and embellishments and the sewing machine.

Metallic Threads and Embellishments

Cut out the leaf without seam allowances and pin or glue-baste it in place. Do not glue in the stitching areas. Set the machine tension for metallic threads; use a neutral-colored, light-weight thread in the bobbin and a machine metalfil needle. A standard needle will break the threads. This is free-form work, and there are no hard and fast rules: What works for you and the sewing machine is your rule. The sample is first outlined, stitched to hold the edges in place, and then satin stitched with metallic thread in a slightly open pattern. The vein is a narrow, lustrous rayon ribbon made for needle-point that is machine couched (over stitched) in place with a two-colored rayon thread. Leave at least 3" tails at both ends so that they can be tied off. The couching thread is also used for the side veins with free-motion stitching. There are many books written on machine decorative stitching and this section gives only a brief overview.

Definition:
Couching is laying a decorative thread on the fabric's surface and attaching it using the same or another thread in a decorative pattern. The machine pattern can be an open zigzag, a more elaborate stitch, or couched by hand.

Free-motion Stitching

❖ Drop the feed dogs of your machine so that the fabric can be moved freely in any direction.

❖ A hoop will help stabilize the work and provide a handle when moving it under the needle.

❖ A darning foot (embroidery foot) helps hold the fabric in place when the needle pulls up and out of the work.

❖ Do use a stabilizer. On the leaf sample, I did not use a hoop, but found that the wash-a-way paper created enough stability that a hoop was unnecessary. However, notice that in photo 5-17, I held the fabric with my fingers close to the presser foot to keep it from pulling up when the needle lifted out of the fabric. Photo 5-18 shows the needle in the up position. Notice how the fabric bulges up slightly. CAUTION: If you use this method, keep your fingers out of the way—or risk piercing your finger with the needle. Ouch!

❖ How to stitch is determined by individual sewing machines. Practice on a small sample before working on the actual block.

❖ Stitch size is created by the speed of the fabric moving under the needle; move it slowly to make tiny stitches and faster for longer stitches.

❖ Relax; this is a free-motion on a leaf. No two are alike; so do not try for balance, which defeats the purpose.

Photo 5-17
Stitching without a hoop. Using stabilizer requires that fingers hold the fabric near the needle. Sew slowly and use caution so your fingers do not get pierced.

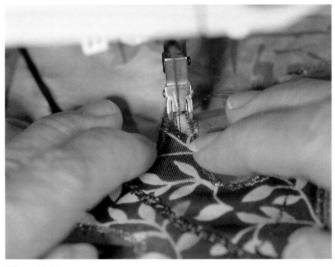

Photo 5-18
The fabric bulges up slightly as the needle comes out of the fabric.

Ending the stem's couched thread is simple and done after all the stabilizer is removed. Thread a large-eyed needle big enough to accept the strand. The needle must make a hole in the leaf and background block so that the thread will pass through to the wrong side without distorting the fabric. Take the thread to the back.

To end a denser thread, weave it on the wrong side the decorative stitch for about an inch. Then reverse the needle, pierce the thread, and weave it back. This eliminates a knot that could leave a bulge showing on the right side of the work. This technique is used in needlepoint, cross-stitch and other embroidery work.

Moss

Various fabrics can be used for the moss. Cut the small patches out and move them around the brick until they are well balanced (refer to Photo 5-2). After the bricks are pressed with the seam allowances going in one direction, needleturn or machine appliqué the moss in place. Here also, decorative threads can be used or embroidery work added.

Snails No More Wall Hanging

Selection of a portion of a pattern and stitching with metallic and rayon threads provides an option to utilize patterns in new and interesting ways. The design is the snail's spiral. The four blocks in the wall hanging are stitched with various threads and stabilizers, but a hoop is mandatory. While a hoop was not used on the quilt example, it did not draw up because there were two layers of fabric under the spiral and a stabilizer. In the wall hanging, there are only two layers: the background block and the spiral. Stitching in circles will cause warping and rippled edges without a hoop and a stabilizer of your choice. A darning foot is recommended.

The Audition: To save time and fabric placement errors, arrange the blocks and audition them for color placement with the 4" fabric squares in place. Try different block and square arrangements until you are satisfied that the colors are balanced.

Photo 5-19
Take the couched thread to the back of the block and weave it through the stitching.

Photo 5-20
Weave it back into the stitching and pierce the thread. No knots are made.

Photo 5-21
The audition of potential spiral fabrics and their arrangement.

YARDAGE AMOUNTS

(All measurements figured on 44" wide fabric)
4 blocks each 8-1/2" square of different fabrics
4 spirals without seam allowances 4" x 4" each of different fabrics (Use the snail spiral
pattern)
Sashing and inner border: Cut three 1-1/2" strips from 44" wide fabric
Narrow border: 3/4" x 21", cut 4
Wide border: 2" x 22", cut 4
Binding: 1" x 23", cut 4. Binding is not doubled.
Finished blocks are 8" square. Cut them 9", complete the stitching, and then recut to size. This is necessary because the blocks may shrink due to dense machine stitching.

Photo 5-22
A piece of contrast fabric with exposed edges turned under can be inserted between the spirals before stitching begins to add color.

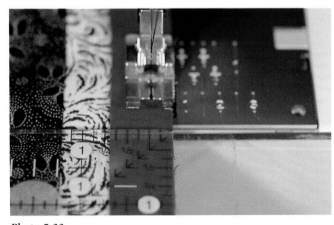

Photo 5-23
Lay the narrow border on top for stitching accuracy.

Cutting the Spirals

Do not layer the spiral fabrics for cutting, as the fabrics will slip. If you choose to fuse the spirals, this is the time to press the product onto the fabric squares. Pin a paper spiral pattern onto the right side of the fabric and cut out the circle.

Remove seam allowances for machine work by cutting on both sides of the spiral line, to create a space a scant 1/4" wide. For needleturn appliqué directions, see pages 18.

Assembly

The spirals can be placed in the same spot on each block, but random placement is more interesting—your choice. Position each spiral and pin, then glue-baste or fuse in place.

Note: If a spiral is picked up, pin mark the location, otherwise you may not remember the placement. I speak from experience!

Sewing

Hand appliqué or back the block with a stabilizer and follow the directions for machine sewing, detailed earlier under The Appliqué Designs. Small folded pieces of contrasting fabric can be slipped under the spirals to provide a color highlight. Machine stitching with various colors and decorative threads adds more sparkle. The samples are stitched with metallic and rayon threads.

Once all four spirals are stitched in place, the resized blocks are joined together with sashing. First, join two blocks with the sash (cut size 1-1/2" x 8-1/2") and repeat for the remaining two blocks. Next, add the center sash that is cut 1-1/2" x 18-1/2".

First, attach the inner borders: Sew 1-1/2" wide strips on top and bottom then add the sides. Next, cut the narrow red border 3/4" wide for a finished width of 1/4". Precise 1/4" seams must be sewn. Lay the narrow border on top to sew.

Hint
Always re-measure and cut the opposite sides to a specific length. They must be the same measurement for the quilt to be square.

Finally, add the outer border that is cut 2" wide. This allows trimming it to 1-1/2" before the binding is added. Attach the border with the narrower one on top. To get exact width of the narrow border, sew with the left side of the presser foot riding along the stitching line.

Press the borders so that the narrow border seam allowances are facing out. Cut the backing and batting an inch larger than the completed top. Pin and baste the unit together in preparation for quilting. Quilt by hand or machine. Because the black and white fabrics are so busy, quilting would not be visible, so everything but the swirls and outer border is stitched in the ditch (directly in the seam lines). The swirls are machine quilted with variegated black and white thread in a pattern that extends the swirl. Quilting patterns and threads are your option. Refer to Chapter 12 for binding instructions (page 114). Finished binding is not doubled.

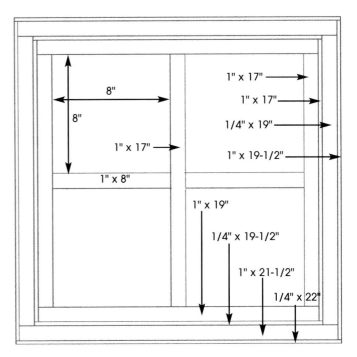

Illus. 5-2
A schematic of the wall hanging.

The Snail No More wall hanging.

ADDITIONAL THOUGHTS

There are several advantages to wash away stabilizers. First, it dissolves quickly without rubbing. This means there is no distortion of the fabric, which is a drawback when removing stabilizers that hold on tenaciously. Also, there is nothing left under the stitching, so the finished work is softer, though it can take longer soaking in warm water for it to dissolve under very dense threads. Yes, wetting the fabric is a nuisance, but I believe this is also an advantage. It allows the fabric to be blocked square if any distortion occurred as a result of the machine work.

With the YLI Wash-A-Way paper, removing the excess paper from around the machine stitching is much easier than with other stabilizers, so there is less dissolving required and larger pieces can be removed for use in other projects.

Try nylon thread pre-wound bobbins for machine embroidery. The thread is wound under pressure and the bobbin has paper sides. It can be used as is, but the better way is to pull off the paper sides. The thread stays together beautifully, is a fine diameter, works like a dream, and is now is available in more colors than white and black.

Bobbin thread must not show on the right side of the fabric. I cannot stress this enough. Therefore, no matter what thread is in the bobbin, the important thing is to have the machine tension adjusted properly and always run a test sample. If the tension does not adjust adequately, have the machine repaired. The ability to adjust and maintain a proper tension is critical.

chapter 6

Pots and Shadows

Photo 6-1
The pots.

MAKING A FLAT SURFACE LOOK ROUND

While traditional artists work with a brush and a favored medium to make flat objects appear curved, quilters are challenged with unique combinations of patterned cloth and shapes. Color selection, design, and cutting mimic the curve, but these are only three items in a quilter's bag of tricks to fool the eye. Adding quilting patterns and, perhaps, applied surface texture into the mix certainly provides an advantage. As you choose fabrics for the pots, keep in mind that the fabric's patterns do not have to be curved. Cutting a linear pattern on the diagonal creates movement and optical illusion. The light source direction is also important.

Photo 6-2
The fabrics.

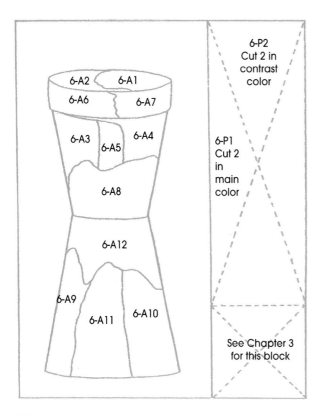

Illustration 6-1
The pots schematic.

POT YARDAGE:

Background block: 8" x 16"

Pot fabrics: Twelve fabric scraps no larger than 4-1/2" x 5" except for 6-A9, which is 6" x 2-1/2"

Pieced Yardage:

6-P1: 6" x 13" rectangle (cut 2) of main color

6-P2: 7" x 7" square (cut 2) of contrasting color
Did you make several 4" squares following the directions in Chapter 3: Quarter-square Triangles, The 1-1/4" Formula? If so, use the extra square here or make one.

How Many Fabrics are Enough?

There are only twelve fabric patches used in this pattern. To create more gradual color changes and the illusion of roundness, divide each patch into smaller shapes. If your option is to add more fabrics, make the divisions on the vertical to enhance the height and curve of the pots. It can be as effective using gradated, hand-dyed or purchased yardage without increasing the number of patches. While there is no right answer to how many fabrics should be used, there is also no wrong answer. How many fabrics you use is a personal preference; choose fabrics that produce the results you want.

Concave Shading

The body of the pot curves forward and the inside upper lip of the pot curves back with reversed shadows and highlights. With the light coming from the right, the lightest areas will be

The black and white drawing was done in a Scientific Illustration class that I took some years ago. Drawn with charcoal on vellum, it depicts a snow goose in flight that is carved from a whale's tooth. The carving was positioned with a strong light angled on the right side. Notice there is no color at the high point at the base of the wing or body, but the curve of the long neck does have some color, however subtle. While this chapter is not intended to teach you how to make a trompe l' oeil or fool the eye image of pots, as in the drawing, do keep in mind that proper placement of light and dark creates curves and depressions, no matter the technique.

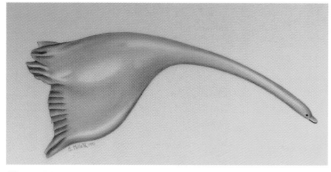

Photo 6-3
A scientific illustration charcoal of an ivory carving by the author.

Photo 6-4
Comparison of both quilt blocks with two different light sources and color schemes.

on the right side of the body and on the inside left edge of the upper lip. For comparison, the block in the traditionally colored quilt has the light source coming from the opposite direction (photo I-2). Study the differences in photo 6-4 before making your fabric selections.

Photo 6-5
Include 1/8" seam allowances on patches that are covered by another patch, but cut without seam allowances at the pattern's edge; see the right side of the template marked "Light."

Appliquéing the Pot

The **What A Garden!** quilt example is more traditional in its needleturn appliqué and hand quilting execution. However, machine appliqué and quilting can be equally successful, as in the example in photo 6-10. By now, you may have settled on an appliqué technique. Consider expanding the stitching options by including free motion or raw edge appliqué. Hand embroidery can accomplish the same look. Below is a list of options that could be used for attaching and stitching the pot's fabric patches.

Choosing Appliqué Options

❖ Fusing the patches in place
❖ Non-fused patches and a non-woven, tear-away stabilizer (the example used this method)
❖ Invisible nylon thread in clear or smoke color
❖ Raw edge appliqué attached with a straight stitch 1/8" from the bias patch's edge
❖ Open zigzag with nylon thread. Do a lock stitch at the beginning and the end, and use the needle-down position

Photo 6-6
In raw edge appliqué, the seams overlap by 1/8".

The example is raw edge appliqué, sewn with a straight stitch and clear nylon thread. Each patch is cut out on the bias to reduce fraying and to take advantage of the fabric's design.

Ignore the fabric's straight-of-grain and choose the fabric design's best angle to enhance your light/dark requirements. The aim is to mimic the pot's curve. Rough cut each patch, but do not trim it close.

As with any appliqué, start at the most distant area and build to the foreground. In this case, 6-A1 goes on first. Trim the patch flush with the top curved back edge, but for the remainder of the oval, leave a 1/8" seam allowance. Place it onto the background block with the top edge even with the pot's top edge. Stitch 1/8" in from the fabric's edge around the entire patch. The seam allowance will lap over into adjoining patches by 1/8". Add patch 6-A2 in the same manner, but overlap the deep concave curve over the oval. Stitch.

Next, add 6-A3. Trim the patch flush with the left side of the pot and leave the other edges extending 1/8" as before. Patch 6-A4 comes next and is trimmed flush on its right side. Stitch. Patch 6-A5 is added next. Notice in the Photo 6-6 how the seams overlap just slightly. Continue on

Hints for Successful Machine Appliqué:
Reduce the straight stitch length to #2 (or about 18 stitches to the inch), and use a #14 embroidery needle. With free-motion stitching, use a darning foot and drop the feed dogs.

Photo 6-7
If heavy texturing is planned, remove a tear-away stabilizer before texturing.

Photo 6-8
The pots with hand quilting that enhances the curved shapes.

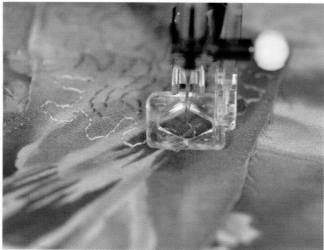

Photo 6-9
A close-up of random texturing the moss.

in this manner, until both pots are completed. Patches 6-A8 and 6-A12 represent moss, so the outside edges do not have to be cut straight. The last piece is 6-A12.

If non-soluble stabilizer was used, remove it now or it will be impossible to take out after texturing is done. Hold your fingers against the stitching line to stabilize it while carefully removing it with the other hand. This prevents twisting the fabric out of shape. This block is especially suited for using water-soluble stabilizer because it does not have to be removed until all stitching is completed. The block is ready for free-motion texture stitching to enhance the curves.

Free-motion Texturing

Free-motion can be done when the block is completed or during the final quilting process. When you add free-motion texture is a personal preference, determined by the look you want to achieve: Thread texture only, or shadow relief created by quilting lines and batting thickness. Photo 6-8 shows hand quilting that has followed the fabric's pattern to create texture and shadow relief from the batting.

The sample in photo 6-9 incorporates thread color and the stitching line to create texture on the block. Here again, there is no right or wrong, only your preference and, frankly, your machine's ability to quilt through layers in short, back-and-forth lines while not leaving a lump of thread on the backing. If you use water-soluble paper, a hoop is not mandatory, but it certainly helps to keep the fabric taut. Gripping the hoop to manipulate the fabric is a definite advantage.

There is no definitive rule for padding a shape to get texture. Most of the sample's stitching is straight line or random. I did not worry about crossing over a stitching line. The point is to bring attention to the highlighted side and the shadowed side, and add curved or angled lines to intensify the pot curves. Just relax, enjoy the freedom of free-motion and don't worry about unequal stitch lengths.

Photo 6-10
The completed pots with machine thread texturing.

Piecing the Rectangle

Follow the directions and illustrations in Chapter 3 to make the triangle and square (page 38). The triangle has different-sized templates, (6-P1 and 6-P2), but the assembly directions are exactly the same. That also applies to constructing the square. See Illus. 3-1 and 3-2 and photos 3-3 to 3-6. Sew the assembled unit onto the pot block.

ADDITIONAL THOUGHTS

The pot block is fairly easy appliqué, whether it is done by machine or hand. Using free-motion stitching may be a new technique to you. Needleturn appliqué is my primary choice, so I do not consider myself an expert at free-motion. That may not be the correct confession for a quilt book author to make, but it is true. As with any technique, it takes time and plenty of experience to learn. I'm learning … and you can, too. What I have found is that relaxing while sewing results in better and more flowing lines … and less neck strain.

Of course, the same points can be made for needleturn appliqué. I tell my students that needleturn produces tension until they learn how to control the seam allowances with the side of the needle. Then it becomes relaxing and fun.

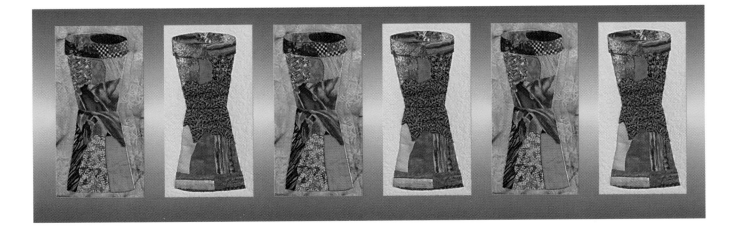

chapter 7

The Onion and Triangles

Photo 7-1
The onion.

The onion is fun to create, and is one of my favorites. In the previous chapter, the use of gradated fabrics was mentioned. In this chapter there are two samples: The **What A Garden!** block, and an example of a single color that ranges from light to dark. The method of appliqué is your decision. The decision on where to place colors and how to compensate for edges that disappear into the background when they should stand out will be explained.

Deciding on Color Placement

Choosing the best fabric for a specific patch is a matter of trial and error. For more experienced quilters, this is an enjoyable process. Many consider it a frustrating one. Ask for help from a shop owner before the joy of playing with color and design is lost. Do keep in mind that when the quilt is viewed as a whole, a small bit of fabric

Photo 7-2
The fabrics.

Onion Yardage

Background block: 8" x 16"

Onion top: 8 fabrics, none larger than 8" x 4"

Onion bulb: 9 fabrics, from long slivers of fabric to 3" x 7-1/2"

Both the onion top and body patches can be cut on the bias

Triangles:

Important Information: These triangles are NOT equilateral triangles; 7-P2R must be turned over before cutting.

7-P1: cut 4 from a brick fabric, 4" x 18" or one fat-eighth

7-P1: cut 3 from a second brick fabric, 4" x 11"

7-P2, 7-P2R: cut 1 each from the second brick fabric, 4" x 5"

Contrasting band: 1" x 16"

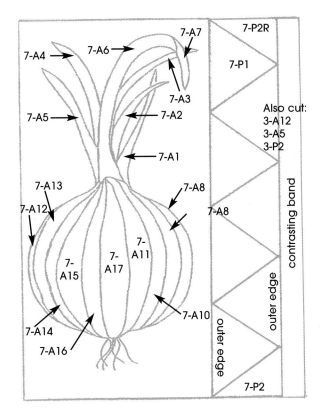

Illus. 7-1
The onion schematic.

that you think is wrong will not change the quilt's overall appearance. That is how I feel about the pear block and the light green triangle on the right side of the background block. With a chance to do it over, I would either repeat that fabric many more times or eliminate it. But I cannot, so I live with it.

The following fabric selection process is the same no matter which design or portion of a design I work on. For instance, nine fabrics are needed for the onion's bulb. Stack possible fabrics, light to dark, with only narrow portions of each showing. After a quick assessment, remove the fabrics that don't fit. Rearrange the pile according to your light source and the order they will be appliquéd. Are you pleased? Is there enough difference between adjacent colors so each is distinct? Step across the room and look at the fabrics. Does the combination still work? Perhaps there might be a better choice for the brightest or lightest fabric. Perhaps one jumps out and seems to say, "Remove me. I don't belong." There is no right or wrong answer to these questions. Each quilter will answer differently.

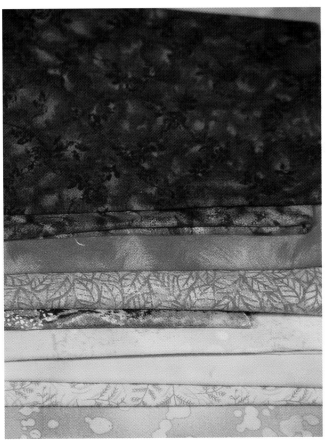

Photo 7-4
The pruned-down choices for the onion.

Photo 7-3
Initial color selections for the onion.

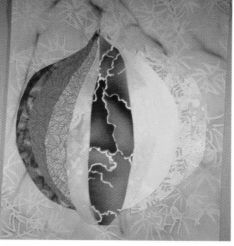

Photo 7-5
This selection needed improvement. The segments on the right are too bland and the center is too strong.

Photo 7-6
The onion's top.

After initial color selections are made, lay them on the back of a chair and look at the arrangement in all types of light. Viewing fabrics at night under artificial light can alter your answers to the above questions.

Once the preliminary choices are made, cut the patches and arrange them in order. Reevaluate the sequence to see that each color works in its assigned place. Perhaps two need to be reversed, or one might not work as a small patch though it looked fine in a larger piece. Study photo 7-5. Yes, the colors blend and there is nothing wrong with the choices, but to my eye, the center is too strong. Study photo 7-1 for the final selection.

By changing only two fabrics, the bulb vibrates and comes to life. The final assessment on whether each color fits comes only after all patches are stitched in place. This happens because the seam allowance widths can fool your perception. There is one exception to this: Fusing. Since these patches are cut out without seam allowance, auditioning is done with finished-size patches and there should be no surprises. The same audition process is used for the onion's top. Using your chosen technique, stitch the top, always working from the back to the foreground.

The Onion Top

I believe it is an instructor's job to tell you what not to do, as well as how to do it correctly. The onion's top fabrics were cut out, glue-basted in place and machine buttonhole stitched with silk thread. Wash-A-Way paper was used as a stabilizer without a hoop. Rather than sew a narrow contrast band in place that is on the edge of the farthest right stem, wooly nylon was zigzagged down the outer edge of the right patch to help define the edge so it would not blend into the background. Here is what I did—and learned not to do.

❖ Glue-baste if desired, but only one leaflet at a time, working from back to front.

❖ Do not use wooly nylon for zigzagging a shadow line. It tends to clump—at least it did for me. Rayon thread would be superior in this application.

❖ Always run a test sample first.

Narrow Contrast Bands

There is an additional concern with this block and how the appliqué fabrics stand out from the background that may not apply to your fabric choices. However, at some point you will encounter this problem. Study photo 7-5. Notice how the appliqué fabric on the far right blends into the background block. After appliquéing, the edge will disappear. It was necessary to remove the patch and insert a narrow band of dark fabric under the outer edge. This is similar to an artist painting a narrow contrasting line on the edge of highlighted objects to separate them from their background. It is close to outlining, but not quite, since darker shadows automatically stand out from the background. An option to adding a contrasting strip of fabric is a row of satin stitching in contrasting thread along the raw edge of the patch.

To add a narrow contrasting band, draw a line a scant 1/8" wide beyond the Master Pattern's outer edge. Only the outer edge of the narrow band is appliquéd. It goes on first and the inside edge's seam allowance is covered by another full patch.

Attach the seam allowance's inner edge with a running stitch to hold it in place (photo 7-7). Stitch over far enough so that it will be covered by the next appliqué. Notice the stitching line for the next patch is already drawn in using a pen for clarity.

Layered Master Patterns

The remaining patterns all have layered appliqué, which requires placing multiple fabrics atop one another. As appliqué patches are added, some of the interior Master Pattern lines are covered. To eliminate guesswork and ease of positioning, use the template to overlay the stitched patch and retrace the hidden line(s).

Place the 7-A8 template and remark its outer stitching line on the contrasting band. Stitch 7-A8 in place. Each time a new patch is applied, the outer edge is appliquéd and the loose seam allowance is held in place with a running stitch and covered by the next appliqué. Continue in this manner until reaching the center patch 7-A17. Both edges of this patch are appliquéd. The onion bulb is complete.

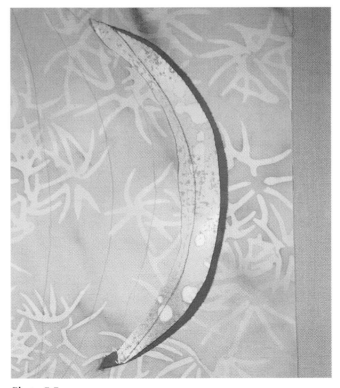

Photo 7-7
A narrow contrasting band has been added a scant 1/8" beyond the edge of the first onion segment.

Photo 7-8
Lay the template over an appliqué to reestablish a hidden line.

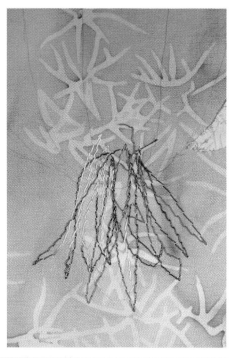

Photo 7-9
Free-motion stitching starts and ends within the body of the onion before appliqué begins.

Photo 7-10
Hold the thread to the side to determine the amount to leave for excess.

Photo 7-11
The completed couched roots using a variegated thread.

The Roots

Consider these two things to determine when to add the roots: Hand or machine work and the technique used. Hand embroidery or quilting the roots is easy to do after the onion is completed. Machine work is better done before the appliqué is completed. This allows the threads to be stitched first, beginning and ending within the body of the onion, to create the feeling that the roots are extending from the bulb. Onion roots are tangled, so the sample in photo 7-9 is free-motion straight stitching done with variegated thread, without a hoop, but with Wash-A-Way Paper for a stabilizer.

The hand-embroidered sample is couched threads. They are stitched after the appliqué is completed. There is no one best choice for couched fibers. This is the time to check your thread stash to see what works with your color scheme. The laid thread is the heavier thread. The thread holding it in place can be the same color, a contrasting color, or metallic, as in the sample.

To begin, use a needle that has an eye that will accommodate the thread. Make a small knot at the end of the thread to be couched down and start it behind the appliqué. Bring the needle to the front of the design just at the bottom edge of the appliqué. Pull the thread through to the surface and stab the needle into the background block where you want the root strand to end. Pull the thread to the back, but leave it loose on the front. Now, bring the thread back to where the next root is to start. Let this thread hang, as it will be used again. Start the couching thread in the same manner and bring it to the surface of the block, just to the side of the thread to be couched and almost touching the appliqué. Now, cross over the larger thread and stab stitch into the background directly opposite where it comes out of the fabric. Pull the thread snug, but not so tight that the couched thread is distorted.

Continue in this manner, pulling/holding the excess couched thread into crooked lines. The couching stitches should be spaced equal distances apart. Continue couching until enough threads have been completed to make it look like a root. The number will vary with the size of the thread being couched in place.

Using Gradated Fabrics

There are a number of companies selling hand-dyed fabrics in eight gradated colors. The advantage is that it takes the guesswork out of selecting a color scheme that blends smoothly from one color or tone to the next. While using the colors as provided is very effective, there is another way to add more vibrancy with the same fabrics: Use the colors out of sequence. The onion's top uses five colors not in sequence. The body has all eight colors, also out of order, adding more movement, depth, shape, and interest. Also, the lightest green on the right of the top blends into the background block, but the choice was to not put in a narrow shadow. Here again, there is no best option. The correct color sequence is what pleases you.

The Triangles

Piecing the triangles can be done by hand or machine. Piecing is handled in the same way as preceding instructions. The caution with shape 7-P2 is that it is not an equilateral triangle. 7-P2R means the pattern is reversed, or turned upside down for cutting. When piecing, have the side of the template marked "Outer Edge" facing out. Marks on the half-triangles indicate which sides are joined to the 7-P1 end triangles. Transfer these marks into the seam allowance before cutting.

Sew the triangles first then add the half-triangles. Do not stitch into the seam allowances. Press the seams so that they all point toward the same direction. Pressing can warp the strip, so be gentle using the iron.

Photo 7-12
The onion using eight gradated fabrics.

To complete the block, stitch the 1" x 16" contrasting band to the right side of the pieced triangles. Piece with the triangles on top so that the seam line crosses at the exact point of each triangle. Sew the pieced strip onto the right side of the onion's background block.

ADDITIONAL THOUGHTS

This chapter is about color placement and being adventurous with its arrangement. Many of us grew up hearing all-knowing adults say that red does not go with pink or that a plaid and print do not go together. As quilters, we can throw those admonitions out the window. Red and pink make a lively combination and adding a plaid to a collection of print fabrics creates interest and movement.

Turn back to the **What a Garden!** quilt, photo I-1. The use of a single strong color—turquoise—in combination with the design carries your eye over the surface of the quilt. It is no accident. Starting on the left, the large triangle to the side of the asparagus points to the triangles under the pear, which brings your gaze inward. The triangles to the right of the pots combine with the contrasting band to carry your vision up into the body of the quilt. Then the block designs help as the daisy and fence move you across the quilt to the peas, which take it down the curving vine to the bottom pea that is angled up. While the pea's flower points to the outside edge, the dragonfly turns your interest back to the interior.

Next, compare it to the quilt in photo I-2.

This was my first effort, using more traditional colors. While the color selections work, the specific changes in the triangles color placement in the **What A Garden!** quilt provide more movement.

The short version is that color and form work together to make a cohesive whole. Rather than trying to assimilate this rather esoteric topic into your fabric selections, just remember to use the same fabric—either bold or muted—for the contrasting bands and triangles. It will work.

Do you hate to rip out, as I do? If you discover that a fabric's edge disappears into a too similar background, your sewing machine can come to the rescue. Couch a row or several rows of contrasting thread along the troublesome fabric to make the design pop.

What if the block tends to ripple even when stabilizer and a hoop were used? Unless it ripples like waves in a storm, there is no problem. Quilting takes care of a multitude of sins. The ripples will flatten out and vanish in a poof—or with multiple rows of machine quilting, to be more precise. That magic comes in the final chapter.

chapter 8

Asparagus

The asparagus stalks are easy to appliqué whichever technique you select. The challenge in this chapter is twofold: Selecting fabrics to create the illusion of a bundle of asparagus with depth, and the small leaflets. On both the quilt examples, the leaflets are hand appliquéd because that is my favored method of working. However, as in the other blocks, there are a variety of options. In this chapter, fusing is the focus and how to overcome the flat, non-dimensional appearance.

Asparagus Yardage

Background block: 8" x 16"
Asparagus stalks: 7 fabrics, each 2" x 14"
Leaflets: Snippets of a variety of fabrics
Tie: 2-1/2" x 5" fabric or a 10" length of heavy cording or narrow trim

Photo 8-1
The asparagus.

Photo 8-2
Traditional asparagus.

Photo 8-3
The fabrics.

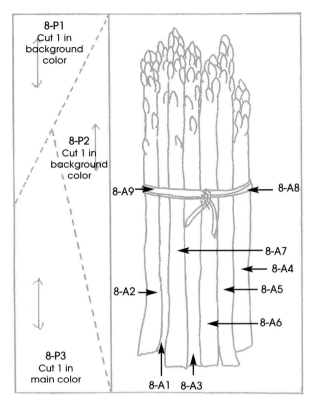

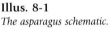

Illus. 8-1
The asparagus schematic.

Oh, Those Stems!

The stems are not difficult, no matter which technique is used to attach them. They are simply straight strips of fabric that can be cut on the straight-of-grain or on the bias to take advantage of a pattern.

How many different fabrics should you use? Study photos 8-1 and 8-2. There are no repeats in the photo 8-1. Each is different. In the traditionally colored quilt, only four fabrics are used. One was repeated three times, another twice and two single fabrics complete the bundle. This was also the first quilt made and an adventurous spirit kicked in for the second.

Creating Depth Using Light and Dark Fabrics

This topic was discussed early in Chapter 7, but it is so important, here is a brief review. There are three things to consider when creating a contoured shape: Distance, light, and dark.

First, distance: The farther away something is, the lighter it becomes. Look at a mountain range or a photograph of one. The mountains can be covered with the same type of vegetation and

trees, but the ones closest are darker and they become lighter the greater the distance. The same color change happens in a cityscape, but it is more subtle. You know that the building farthest away is a dark color, but it will appear lighter the more you travel away from it. Distance affects color.

Bringing in a light source to create highlights and shadows adds to the problem, because logic tells you that the asparagus stalk farthest away from the light source will be darkest and the stalks closest to the light are highlighted. The dilemma is that in order to make the bundle appear curved, the center stalk closest to you needs to be dark since it is in the foreground, yet a stalk on the lightest side must be behind others to make the optical illusion of the curve. It is easiest to accomplish this when using a single color scheme, as in photo 8-2. Here, the center stalk comes forward and is dark. Ideally, the fabric should be shaded on its left side (remember, on this quilt the light source is from the left.) The forward-most stalk is also darker than the one on the far right which is in full shadow. This pushes the illusion of depth.

Now look at photo 8-1. The center stalk is a rippled orange, yellow, and teal and sits between two different bright orange/yellow fabrics. Because of the pattern and the teal, the center stalk visually moves behind the two stalks on either side. The red stalk on the right moves forward because of its richer tone. Isn't it interesting what happens—frequently by accident?

It is absolutely necessary to arrange your stalk fabrics on a board or a vertical surface so that you can stand back to see what is happening. Looking at the results up close does not work. The directions below tell how to make a design board.

Constructing a Design Board

Purchase:
1/2" thick foam core board, 20" x 30"
Medium gray cotton fabric approximately 24" x 34" to cover the board
Short, sharp straight pins with a 1" shaft and glass heads

This compact design wall is easily stored. The photographs for *Quilting the Savory Garden* were taken using it as a background. Do not use a white cover as it is too distracting and draws your eye away from the design. Gray is a better choice. I prefer pins to attach the fabric. This board is easy to pin patches onto or to mount fabric temporarily with double-faced tape. If the gray fabric becomes loose when the mounting tape is removed, simply remove a pin, tighten the fabric, and re-pin.

Wash the fabric to remove the sizing and press. Lay the fabric on a flat surface and center the foam core board on it. Starting in the center of one long side, pull the fabric over the edge, fold the raw edge in and pin the fabric to what will be the backside of the board. The pins must go in at an angle or they will pierce through to the surface. Pin every inch down one long side, keeping the raw edges straight. Move to the opposite side and repeat the process. Pull the fabric taut enough so that it is slightly stretched. Next, move to one end. Fold each corner in as if making bed corners and repeat the pinning process. Finish the fourth side. Check that the fabric is taut, but not distorted. The board is ready to use.

Applying Color Theory

How do you put these rather confusing color theories into practice? Begin by cutting the darkest darks and the lightest lights in your color scheme. Mount them on the board in their approximate locations—no Master Patterns needed; just stick them up in their approximate locations. Next, cut the center stalk. Put it in place.

Cut the remaining fabrics and apply them to the board. Step away and squint. Or take the entire board—oops, you better stab-pin into each stalk before you move the board—and hold it up to a mirror to see the reflection.

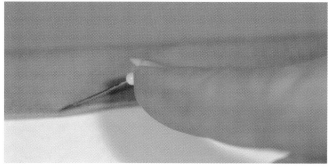

Photo 8-4
Pull the fabric to the reverse side of the board; fold the edge under and pin into the board at an angle.

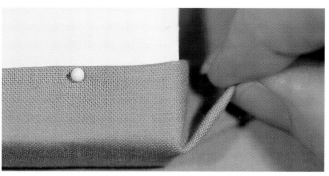

Photo 8-5
Fold the fabric around each corner so there is little bulk, and pin.

Photo 8-6
Start auditioning fabrics by cutting the lightest and darkest fabrics.

Hint
I use the mirror-viewing trick to study all my work, both in process and completed.

Alert
Read "Applying a Tie to Hold a Fabric Bundle," on page 83, before fusing or sewing the outermost stalks.

Photo 8-7
The completed stem selection before stitching.

Keep arranging and changing fabric strips until you are pleased with the combination. Do not spend hours on this process. You can end with enough fabric strips to fill a bathtub, become totally confused, and still not make a decision. Realize that color selection can be the most frustrating part of the quilt making process, and on any given day choices may be different. Once completed, each fabric selection becomes a part of the blended, unified quilt.

Fusing the Stalks

Using your favorite fusing product, attach the stalks to the background block. Follow the template numbers for the correct order. When fusing, I lap edges. This means that stalks 8-A2, 8-A6 and 8-A7 will have no side seams. The stalk on the far right (8-A4) will not have an outside seam, but will have a seam on its left side so that it can be covered by 8-A5. Once all the stalks are fused, it is time to finish the edges so that fraying is eliminated. Notice in photo 8-8 that the tops are not pointed, but will be covered by leaflets.

Leaflets—Fusing and Needleturn Appliqué

Cut out the leaflets from a variety of fabrics, removing seam allowances for fusing, but include them for needleturn appliqué. It is not necessary to make templates, just use the pattern as a guide and cut freehand so that they are different sizes. Choose contrasting colors for the leaflets so that they will stand out from the stalks.

If fusing, cut the leaflets without seam allowances and apply them, following the pattern. Notice that the stalks have been cut slight-

Photo 8-8
Stalks are fused and free-form stitching of leaflets is in process.

ALERT! READ THIS BEFORE FUSING:

Test a sample of single and layered fused fabrics to make sure the fusing product works as advertised and is compatible with your machine. It can gum up the needle and/or cause skipped stitches and broken threads. A single layer of fused fabric may be all right, but problems can arise when sewing through multiple layers of fused fabrics. If this happens, try other fusing products or a different technique.

The sample is satin stitched with rayon threads in varying colors using a machine embroidery needle. Notice that the third stalk from the right is edge stitched with two different colors. Stitching down the left, shadowed side looked wrong using a light thread. It was removed for a darker color that emphasizes that side is away from the light. Use a stabilizer to prevent the fabric from rippling for machine work. Buttonhole stitching and needleturn appliqué are also good options.

ly short of their pointed ends to reduce bulk. The leaflets form the stalk points. Once the tiny shapes are arranged to your satisfaction, fuse them in place.

An alternative to fusing is to straight stitch around the leaflets to hold them in place, followed by decorative edge stitching or random straight stitching, as in photo 8-8.

For needleturn appliqué, cut, including a seam allowance that is less than 1/4", each leaf. Position as many or few as you like. It is not necessary to transfer pattern lines. Appliqué referring to the photos to the right. Also refer to photo 8-1 or the pattern for approximate placement locations. Begin appliqué on the convex (outer) curve away from the corner. Remember, never begin needleturn at a corner, point, or tight curve.

Turn the point as instructed in Chapter 3, Points, photos 3-24 to 3-26 (page 44). Points on the leaflets need not be very sharp. Notice that the top of the stalk is not turned under, but basted across. This reduces bulk when leaflets are appliquéd over the tip.

Appliqué down the remaining side, trimming as you go. The bottom of the leaflet just needs to be tucked under in a straight fold. Finish the stitching by sewing back up to the start.

Applying a Tie to Hold the Bundle

The decision on what to use for tying the bundle needs to be made before sewing the outer stalks. The options are many: Fabric, cording, flat trims, and ribbons. Just be sure that anything selected is machine washable and will not bleed. Because round cording and trims can fray when cut, lay the ends under the both sides of the bundle's outer stalks before the stalks are stitched, especially if machine stitching. A fabric tie is appliquéd last.

The sample is needleturn appliqué. Each round was cut from fabric and appliquéd in the traditional manner. The ends were appliquéd next and topped with the knot. Another option is to make a bias fabric cording. The seam allowance is enough stuffing. It is then appliquéd in place by hand. The ends are tucked under and appliquéd in from both sides

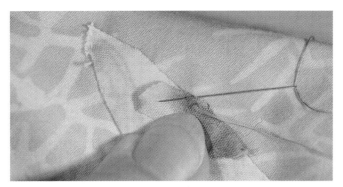

Photo 8-9
Needleturn appliqué of a leaflet starts at the center of a long side.

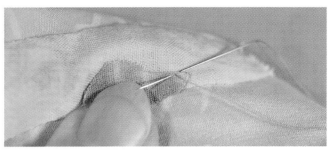

Photo 8-10
Work toward the point and down the other side.

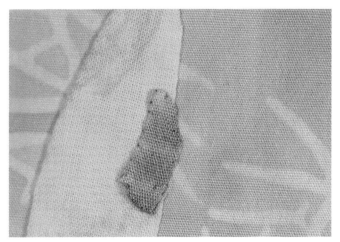

Photo 8-11
A completed leaflet shows the flat bottom that is just folded under before stitching.

Photo 8-12
This tie bundle is needleturn appliquéd.

Photo 8-13
Red trim is attached at both ends before the outer stalks are stitched. Once the stalks are sewn, flip the trim into place and whipstitch down.

Pieced Triangles

Complete the pieced block with the patterns provided. Join 8-P2 to 8-P3, then add 8-P1. Sew it to the completed asparagus block.

ADDITIONAL THOUGHTS

As an option for hand appliqué or embroidery, machine embellishment can create a variety of textures in the blocks. Be sure to experiment using a small swatch. This allows you to adjust your machine's tension, determine the best stitch style, size, length, and width for each design. Here again, there is no one best technique or thread, only what you prefer. It is vital to make fusing samples until a combination of product, layering, and machine compatibility meld together to produce a quality appliqué.

Keep in mind that layering fabrics and adding lots of decorative machine stitching will draw up the background block, so both a stabilizer and hoop are essential. One way to overcome this problem is to cut the background block 1/2" larger on all sides, complete the stitching, press the block, and re-cut to size.

until close to the center. Make the knot and complete the appliqué.

Using purchased trim is easy. Attach the two ends under opposite sides of the bundle. Complete the stalk appliqué. Next, stitch the tie sewing toward the center, then cut the tie to length, knot it, and complete the stitching. This way, the knot lays flat and its position is adjustable. An option is to make the knot first and appliqué the tie using your preferred method.

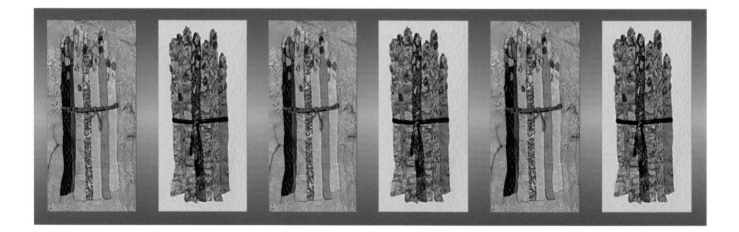

chapter 9

Peppers

Photo 9-1
The peppers.

Photo 9-2
The fabrics.

PEPPER YARDAGE:

Background block: 8" x 20"
Peppers: 15 bottom segments, each about 2" x 6-1/2"
13 top segments, each about 1-1/4" x 2" or smaller
Stems: 3 stems, 1-1/4" x 1-1/2"; 2 stem tops, snippets of fabric

A row of peppers in hot, vibrant colors or realistic tones is eye catching, and presents a wonderful experiment in utilizing the fabric's surface design to enhance the vegetable's bumps and depressions. Here again, this design challenges you to explore fabrics and to visualize portions of a print for one of the pepper's segments. Expand your horizons and look for big, bold designs, large florals, and unusual geometric shapes. Once appliquéd in place, these decidedly nontraditional prints provide movement and create shape, which can be better choices than tiny repeat prints.

Creating Dimension Using Fabric Patterns

In the preceding chapter on the asparagus, the emphasis was on the use of light and dark fabrics. Now, the focus is on using a fabric's pattern to further develop the shapes into three-dimensional objects. The two—color and fabric design—go hand-in-hand and cannot be divorced.

Selecting just the right fabric based on a particular shape may add a new element to quilt making that you have not explored.

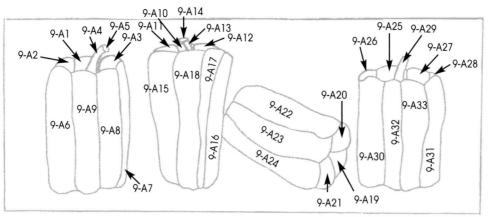

Illustration 9-1
The peppers schematic.

Paying attention to what unique curl, linear pattern, or line creates the perfect shape adds a sense of adventure when combing through your stash or a store's inventory. It also makes your fabric selections look like they were attacked by scissors run amok. The happy thought is that it frequently makes shopping a necessity to locate just the ideal design element in a fabric's repeat pattern.

Some of the samples in photo 9-3 were used in the peppers. The top left dark blue fabric is in the second pepper from the left in photo 9-1.

When fabrics are cut apart, the tiny selections take on an identity separate from the original. A highlighted leaf half creates a more lifelike appearance when another fabric is used for the lower half rather than using an entire leaf. In photo 9-4, the upper center blue fabric looks like a bird's body, but it could just as well be cut in half and used as a fish fin. The red, orange, and yellow fabric looks like strokes

Photo 9-3
A selection of interesting prints for fussy-cutting as in those to the right, photo 9-4.

Photo 9-4
Fussy-cut prints can be adapted for many appliqué shapes.

from a paintbrush and is a favorite that reappears throughout the **What A Quilt!** blocks.

Remember that seam allowances must be added to any fussy-cut fabric so the outer edges of the shape must be predetermined. Use a see-through template of the actual size shape with the seam allowance included. It is laid over the fabric, moved about until the design is positioned properly. The cutting line is marked and the patch cut.

Appliquéing the Peppers

Prepare the background block for appliqué as in prior blocks and cut out the patches. As with all appliqué, start building the design from the back to the front. The pepper tops will be attached first, stems next, and the body of the peppers last. Patch 9-1A can be cut in one piece so that it extends the short distance to the right of the stem (photo 9-6). Cut out the stem, making sure that its base is left long enough to extend under and be covered by the top of the pepper segments in the body of the vegetable.

Stuffing the Stem

Making the stem stand out in relief is easy. It can be accomplished in two ways: Applying batting behind the shape as in Chapter 2, the Flower. Refer to An Easy Option to Create Dimension on page 34. Another option is to stuff the shape before the appliqué is completed. Begin by stitching around the entire stem, but leave the bottom end open. Lightly stuff the stem, poking in small amounts of batting rather than trying to shove in a large wad at once. Smooth out the batting so that it is filled evenly then sew a row of running stitches to close the stem's bottom.

Appliqué the top of the stem by making an oval as detailed in Chapter 4: Ovals and Circles (page 51). The oval is cut a scant 5/8" by 6/8".

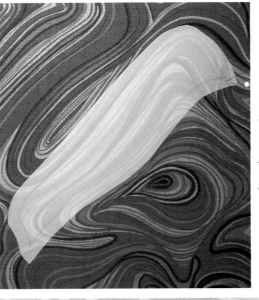

Photo 9-5
A see-through template positioned on fabric to audition it for fussy-cutting.

Photo 9-6
Patch 9-1A is appliquéd and marked for sewing the remaining patches.

Photo 9-7
The stem is stuffed through the bottom and then closed with a running stitch.

HINT:
Having trouble seeing to cut a pencil line on the matte Mylar™? Place a piece of white paper behind it. Cut the two as a single unit and throw the paper away—no more guessing where a pencil line is drawn.

Photo 9-8
The completed stuffed stem with its top appliquéd in place.

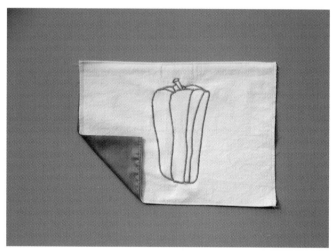

Photo 9-9
Pocket for canvas tote bag is decorated with a pepper outline stitched with metallic thread, then lined.

TOTE BAG YARDAGE:
(enough fabric for two totes)

1-1/3 yards of 45" wide canvas or similar sturdy fabric
1-1/3 yards of 45" wide lining (optional)
4 yards of strapping for handles per bag
Hook & loop tape (optional) to close pocket: 4", enough for two pockets
Cut the canvas and lining fabric into two 36" x 22" rectangles. The 12" x 45" piece is for pockets.

Once gathered, the seam allowance acts as stuffing and nothing more needs to be added. Do not sew through to the background block when stitching over the stem; catch only the stem fabric.

Adapting Patterns for Other Uses

The patterns in *Quilting the Savory Garden* can be adapted for many uses other than quilts, providing the opportunity to work through a design and adapt it to your methods before committing to a large quilt project. You also can audition fabrics and threads to see if they work as you envisioned—a perfect way to tell if something needs to be changed before making a multi-yard fabric purchase. Consider kitchen curtains edged with a row of colorful peppers, a vest with a strand of peas dangling over the shoulder, or a little girl's dress with miniature flowers marching along its hem. And what quilter ever has enough tote bags? The sample bag demonstrates another adaptation for a pattern design by using only the outline.

Making the Outer Pocket

❖ Cut canvas and lining fabrics each 9-1/2" x 12". Lay the lining aside.

❖ Transfer a single pepper pattern to the canvas using the Master Pattern technique.

❖ Machine outline stitch the design in the thread of your choice. The sample is a metallic.

❖ Use a stabilizer under the canvas to prevent warping of the fabric.

❖ Put the completed canvas pocket right sides together with the lining.

❖ Stitch only the top and bottom with 1/2" seams. Do not stitch the sides. This makes a tube.

❖ Turn the pocket right side out. Finger-press the stitching lines and outline stitch the top and bottom edges.

❖ Center a napped length of hook and loop tape on the lining near the top edge and stitch it in place.

Making the Tote Bag

Serge, zigzag, or fold over the edge and top stitch the 22" canvas ends. Serge or zigzag the sides, if you choose. Form the end gussets so that the bag has a flat bottom.

❖ With the bag inside out, finger press one seam allowance flat and position the fabric flat so that it forms a triangle.

❖ Mark 2" away from the point of the triangle and draw a straight line across the bag.

❖ Make sure that this line is at right angles to the seam line.

❖ Stitch two or three rows on the line to reinforce the corner.

❖ Cut 1/4" outside the stitching.

❖ Repeat for the other side.

Turn the bag right side out. Repeat the above steps for the lining, but leave it wrong side out once it is completed. Insert the lining into the bag with wrong sides together. Fold over the top edge about 1" and stitch down. The lining could be trimmed off by 1", but leaving it in place creates a little extra stability and stiffness for the bag's opening.

Next, attach the pocket's hooked tape to the bag. Find the center of one long side and place the hooked tape down about 3" from the bag's opening, or at the distance you prefer. Stitch the hooked tape in place. Press the pocket in place and pin the outer edges. Now make the placement decisions for the straps.

Pin on the strap loops and try the bag on for size. Is the loop so long that when it is over the shoulder you cannot reach items in the bag? Too short? Spaced far enough apart? The answers to these questions will differ with each person. Generally, the strap loops will measure 20" to 22" and will be placed 4-1/4" in from each side. Also consider if the bag will drag on the ground if it is held in your hand. This was the deciding factor for me to make strap loops at 20".

The pocket is big enough to provide gener-

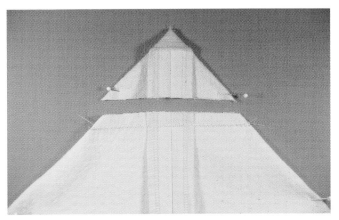

Photo 9-10
The bag corner marked and stitched, with the excess cut off.

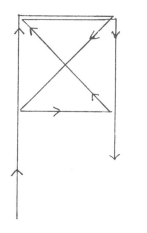

Illus. 9-2
"Z" stitching pattern to reinforce the straps.

ous room to hold quilting necessities. The strap is applied in one continuous length so that there is only one seam to join on the underside of the bottom. Pin the outer edge of one strap in place and sew it down around the entire bag. Lay the pocket's unattached edge under the unstitched edge; trim length if necessary. Pin in place and stitch so that the raw edge is under the strap and securely attached. Repeat for the remaining strap and pocket side.

While stitching the strap to the bag, reinforce each of the four straps at the top edge of the bag. The reinforced stitching can be done in one unbroken line by following Illustration 9-2.

Another lined pocket can be sewn inside on the bag's remaining side. Make it the same size or smaller, only finish all the sides. With hook and loop tape added, an inside pocket is a secure place to store your wallet or checkbook when venturing out to a quilt show.

The completed tote bag.

Finally, the bottom edge of the pocket needs to be sewn. If it is too long, take a tuck in the bottom edge, or if the excess is slight, work it in. The amount of excess will vary for each person depending on strap placement. Stitch across the base. The bag is complete.

ADDITIONAL THOUGHTS

There are many creative ways to construct and decorate your tote bag. Consider changing both the height and width to meet your specific needs. Any of the blocks from *Quilting the Savory Garden* would make delightful bag embellishments. Sew it to a sturdy base fabric before constructing the bag itself. Perhaps you want several interior pockets. Make adaptations accordingly. I wanted something more decorative than plain canvas straps, so large rickrack was sewn to the strap's surface. It provides more body and a unique look. The bag is a perfect container to carry your quilting-in-process for the remaining two blocks.

chapter 10

Fence and Daisy

Photo 10-1
Fence and daisy block.

Photo 10-2
The fabrics.

This chapter combines two different designs into a large, unusual-shaped block with a daisy that extends into three sections. The daisy should present few problems, as it is made of large leaves and easy appliqué shapes for the petals. However, part of the daisy's design is appliquéd to a pieced strip of triangles. The fence looks more difficult than it is because of the narrow strips of fabric representing the slat's edges. There are other options to appliquéing these narrow pieces, so here again, you can choose the method that works best for you. Block assembly is rather unusual in order to join the pieces.

Marking the Master Pattern for the Fence and Daisy

This chapter includes an overview of construction for the entire design. First, the fence design is marked and appliquéd, using your favored method, onto a 20"-long block. An option is to split the fence block into two: 4" x 8" (joined to the daisy section) and 16" x 8" (fence and a portion of the leaf). The triangles are pieced and the contrasting

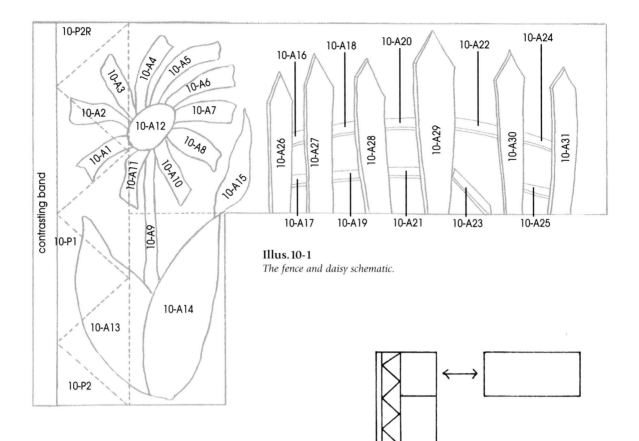

Illus. 10-1
The fence and daisy schematic.

Daisy and Fence Yardage

Background blocks:
Flower: 4" x 8" (lower right corner)
Fence: 8" x 20"
10-P1, 10-P2, 10P2R triangles: two strips of different brick colors, each 4" x 14"
Contrasting band: 1" x 16"
Flower Appliqué Fabrics:
Flower Leaves: 4" x 8", 4" x 9", 2-1/4" x 5"
Stem: 1" x 6-1/2"
Center: 2-1/2" x 2-1/2"
Petals: 10 fabrics, none larger than 3" x 3-1/2"
Fence Appliqué Fabrics: Left to right, 6 slats
10-A26, 1-1/2" x 6-1/2"
10-A27, 1-3/4" x 7-1/2"
10-A28, 1-3/4" x 7-1/2"
10-A29, 2-1/4" x 8-1/2"
10-A30, 1-3/4" x 7-1/2"
10-A31, 1-3/4" x 6-1/2"
Rails: 10 fabrics, none larger than 1" x 3".
    Templates are not necessary.
Slat edges: 22 narrow strips, none larger than 1/2" x 7". Templates are not necessary.

Illus. 10-2
Two options for assembly of the blocks before the daisy appliqué is done.

band is added to it. The triangle unit is joined to the lower and upper daisy block. There are two ways to join these blocks together; no single way is better than the other. The daisy is marked and appliquéd.

Once the entire large block is assembled, mark the daisy onto the fabric using your preferred method: Master Pattern, overlay, plunk & pin. Refer to photo 10-1 and illus. 10-2 to see how the daisy design extends into all the sections except the contrasting band to the left of the triangles. When transferring a Master Pattern design to the strip of triangles, treat the strip as if it is a single layer of fabric.

The Fence

Cut out the fence block and mark the design on the right side of the fabric using your preferred method. Color choices for the slats and their edges pose some interesting questions. I handled them differently on each of my quilts. The traditional quilt uses the same fabric in each slat: A basket weave for the slats, another for the long ends, and a third highlight color for the top ends. In this quilt, the light comes from the top left.

The **What a Garden!** fence follows the fabric-selection philosophy that more color and prints are better. Here, all three sides, slats, and side and top ends are different. See photo 10-1.

It is not necessary to make templates for the ends or short connecting rails. Just cut long, narrow bias strips. Straight-of-grain does not matter for any of the fence patches. In this instance, selecting the best position for the fabric's design is of primary importance.

The Rails—Machine

It is fastest to sew the fence in an assembly line by stitching the cross rails first then the slats. Cut a cross rail on the bias, including end seam allowances, lay it over the upper Master Pattern line with the top seam allowance folded under, and a piece of stabilizer under the background fabric. Using a clear or smoke-colored monofilament thread, machine straight stitch the top edge of the rail in place with a slightly shortened stitch length (#2). Lift the patch up, and trim the seam allowance to 1/8" (photo 10-4). Repeat for the top of all side rails.

Trim the bottom of the rail fabric so it falls within the two pencil lines that depict the rail's edge. Put a decorative thread in the machine. The example uses rayon thread. With water-soluble paper as a stabilizer, it is not necessary to work in a hoop. However, it does help to place your index and middle fingers on either side of the fabric in a "V" and apply slight outward tension. The right hand is now free to change the machine settings.

Machine straight stitch 1/16" from the edge of the fabric to hold it in place for satin stitching. With the needle down, rotate the block and change the machine's controls for a close satin stitch. Satin stitch back over the straight stitching. This stitching should cover the fabric's cut edge and the straight stitches. The width can be varied from 2.5 to 3.5 as you are sewing.

Photo 10-3
The traditionally colored fence using a basket weave fabric.

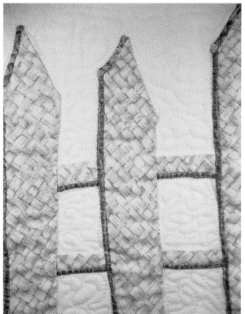

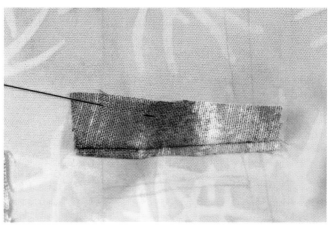

Photo 10-4
Hand or machine stitch along the top edge of the rail. Trim the seam allowance. Flip the rail right side up into position.

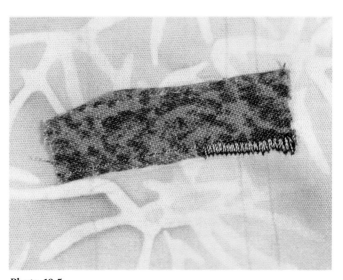

Photo 10-5
Both edges can be machine stitched. The topstitching is monofilament and the bottom is satin stitched with rayon.

Photo 10-6
Machine stitch the first side along the edge from bottom to top. Rotate the block and satin stitch down and over the straight stitching.

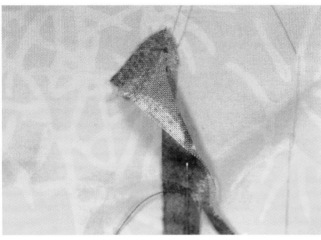

Photo 10-7
The right side is attached with a running stitch. Trim and attach the loose side with a running stitch.

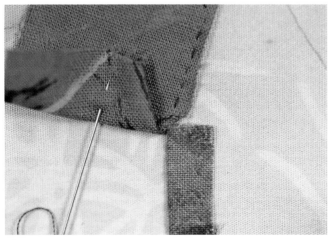

Photo 10-8
Attach the top with a running stitch. Fold the bottom up at an angle.

The Slats—Machine

For machine work, fold under the seam allowance on the right side and pin the slat in place. Straight stitch close to the folded edge with monofilament. Fold in the point. Change to a decorative thread. Straight stitch 1/16" in from the raw edge from the slat's bottom to the top edge. At the point, with the needle down, rotate the entire block. Reset the machine controls to a satin stitch. If you are using only one color, taper the zigzag from small to normal width, and continue stitching down the side into the seam allowance.

If two colors are used, satin stitch up the slat's side to the angled turn and end the thread. Change thread colors and stitch from the point, beginning with several lock stitches, down to where it connects with the satin stitching. Overstitch several threads and lock stitch to secure the ends. Repeat until all slats are completed.

The Slats—Needleturn Appliqué

Needleturn appliqué the slat's long narrow edge first. Begin on the left side (see Chapter 3: Narrow Stems, page 42) with a running stitch, start at the top, leaving a 1/4" seam allowance, sew to the block's bottom, end the thread and trim the seam allowance.

Stitch across the bottom in its seam allowance and come back up the right side with a running stitch to its top. Do not fold in the end. (see photo 10-8.) Cut the pointed edge 1/2" longer than the actual design. This allows ample fabric to fold in both ends. Use the same running stitch technique to sew on the first side of the top down to cover the long edge. Double fold the bottom edge. Do not trim the excess yet.

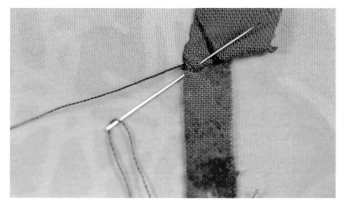

Photo 10-9
Stitch the edge in place.

Photo 10-10
Expose the wrong side of the fabric and fold the point down to form the tip of the point. Trim where necessary.

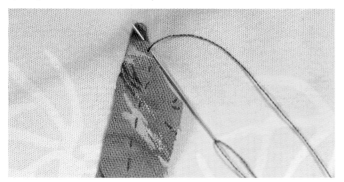

Photo 10-11
Fold in to form the point and stitch in place.

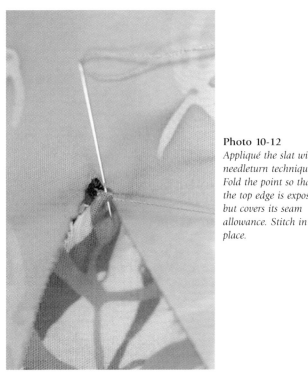

Photo 10-12
Appliqué the slat with needleturn techniques. Fold the point so that the top edge is exposed, but covers its seam allowance. Stitch in place.

Photo 10-13
The completed top of the fence.

Now, roll the fabric right side up. This is important: Check that the fold looks okay, trim away the excess fabric, but leave a seam allowance of 1/4" extending to the right.

Open the fabric back up and, with the needle's tip, tuck the top excess in to form the top of the point.

Hold the point in place and complete the running stitches, then stitch the point in place. Trim away excess seam allowance.

The slat is stitched from the right bottom up to the point (for left-handed stitchers, start at the bottom left corner). Flat fold the first corner and appliqué up to the point. Fold in the point and trim as necessary. Refer to Chapter 2: Points (page 33) to review instructions.

Continue appliquéing down the remaining side, trimming the seam allowance as necessary. The bottom of the fence extends into the block's seam allowance, so it does not have to be appliquéd. Just hold it in place with a running stitch in the seam allowance.

Photo 10-14
The overlap of the daisy's right leaf.

The Pillow:

Background block for appliqué: 9" x 17" (includes 1/2" seam allowances)
Stabilizing muslin fabric: 9" x 17"
Backing fabric: 9" x 17"
Trim: 2 yds

Piecing the Triangles

Piecing the triangles is the same as detailed in Chapter 7, illus. 7-1, page 73). Have the long edges of the triangles on the fabric's straight-of-grain. This helps in stabilizing the outer edges of the strip to prevent stretching. Press gently. All the accuracy in cutting and piecing can be undone with a heavy hand on the iron. Finally, add the contrasting band to the left side of the pieced triangles. Sew with the triangles on top so that the points are visible and stitching does not cut them off. Press the unit and set aside.

The Flower

The entire fence-daisy block must be assembled before marking the Master Pattern daisy pattern on the fabric. In the schematic and pattern, the dashed lines behind the daisy indicate the pieced triangles. Constructing the daisy itself is straightforward. It can be machine satin stitched, buttonholed, or needleturn appliquéd following the directions in preceding chapters.

No matter which technique is used, the stem goes on after 10-A9 and the bottom petal (10-A11) is last. The seam allowance at the top point of the large leaf on the right (10-A14) is not turned under. The top leaf segment (10-A15) overlays the top of 10-A14.

Constructing the Fence Pillow

Cut out the background and transfer the pattern to the right side using your preferred method. Complete the appliqué. Machine baste the muslin stabilizing fabric to the back of the appliquéd block with a 1/2" seam allowance. If you choose, measure 1-1/2" out from each corner and draw a diagonal line between these points. This eliminates applying bulky trim to the right angle corners, and gives the pillow a rounded appearance.

The fence pillow.

Never start applying a trim at a corner, as it makes it harder to make a seamless joint. To prevent the fringe from raveling, zigzag the end that will be attached first. First, determine which is the trim's right side. Sometimes it does not matter. Apply the trim to the background block, right sides together, along its bottom edge about 3" away from a corner with the top of the trim within the seam allowance. Stitch around the entire background block and stop about 6" away from the joining. Measure the length of trim needed to butt the ends together. Zigzag the end and cut off the excess. Complete stitching the trim to the block.

Pin the backing fabric and completed top right sides together. Be careful that the trim is not caught by the stitching in the seam allowance. Stitch together, leaving a 6" opening. The machine's tension may have to be loosened so that the stitching does not pull the seam line out of shape. Stuff the pillow with small hand-fuls of polyester fiberfill. This makes a smoother finished appearance. Hand whipstitch the opening closed.

ADDITIONAL THOUGHTS

The fence pattern lends itself to a variety of uses. It makes the perfect solution to enlarging the quilt, or decorate a garment's sleeves with the fence. There is a caution when decorating garments. Watch the placement of embellishments or risk a disaster. Bust points are a no-no and a fence enclosing your hips is probably not advisable unless you wear a size 2. To take the guesswork out of placement, cut out the pattern and drape it on your body, then avoid pining the appliqué in the problem area.

The next chapter details the sweet pea block, how to assemble the blocks into the completed top, and how to prepare and turn the fabric sandwich into a quilt.

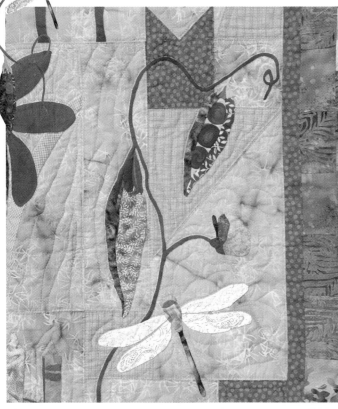

chapter 11

Pea Pods, Vines, Dragonfly

Photo 11-1
The upper sweet pea blocks.

Photo 11-2
The lower sweet pea blocks. Notice how the dragonfly tail and vine cross the seam lines.

Photo 11-3
The fabrics.

This is the final set of designs in *Quilting the Savory Garden*. Nine blocks form the entire right lower portion of the quilt and use techniques covered in earlier chapters. In this chapter, you will construct the pod, the dragonfly, and assemble the blocks. While the yardage amounts look confusing, the entire design is comprised of various sized blocks that are pieced or appliquéd, then stitched together. The pea fabric might send you on a shopping quest. While it is not necessary to use a fabric with a circular design, it does enhance the pea's shape. However, shaded fabrics work especially well since the peas can be fussy-cut to position highlights and shadows. The design can also stand-alone and will make an eye-catching wall hanging that only requires a border to finish it.

Pea Pods Block Yardages

Background blocks:
11-P6: cut three 4" x 4" squares
8" x 16" rectangle
4" x 16" rectangle
11-P1: cut two 4" x 8-1/8" x 8-1/8" triangles
11-P2: cut two 8-1/4" x 8-1/4" x 16"
triangle with 16" length on straight-of-grain

Use the same patterns from the pear chapter:
3-P2 and 3-P3: 2 quarter square triangles
3-P1: cut 4 patches, 3 of one color and 1 of a second color

The shapes below comprise one 8" x 16" finished rectangle:
11-P5: cut one 8" x 9" x 12" triangle
11-P3: cut one 7-1/2" x 11-1/2" x 16" triangle (16" length on the straight-of-grain)
11-P4: cut one 7" x 4-1/2" x 11-1/2" x 8" shape

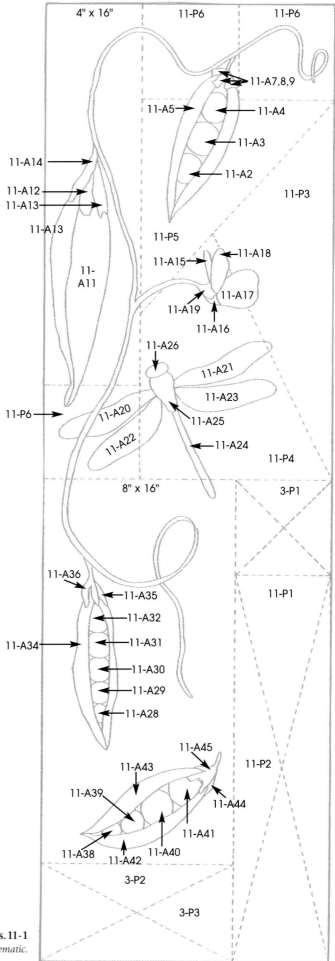

Illus. 11-1
The pea pods schematic.

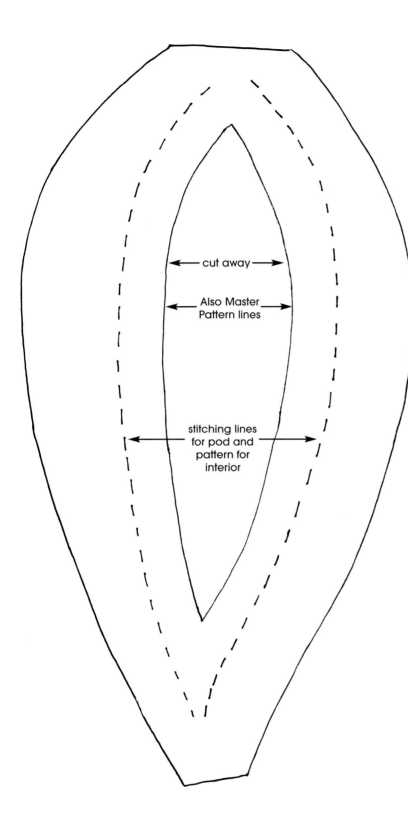

Illus. 11-2
Template option for the pea pod.

cut away

Also Master Pattern lines

stitching lines for pod and pattern for interior

Laying the Pattern and Assembling the Block

Portions of the appliqué are done first and some of the designs (vine, upper pea pod, and dragonfly) cross seam lines. The curving vine can be appliquéd free form without a pattern. Just stitch it where you want it to go between the pods. The other option is to lay a Master Pattern. If you use this method, *do not* draw the pencil lines right up to the seams, but stop 1/2" away. This eliminates the problem of pencil lines not meeting exactly when the blocks are joined.

The upper section is easy if taken in steps. Piece the blocks that form the right section (11-P3 to 11-P6) and add the two blocks on the left side. Lay the Master Pattern on this section. Assemble the lower pieced blocks and one large block then trace the Master Pattern on it. Appliqué the large pods. Join the two sections and appliqué the vine. Appliqué directions follow.

Pea Pods

Appliquéing the two-colored pea pods on the **What a Garden!** quilt is similar to techniques detailed in preceding chapters. Baste the pod's back to the background block and appliqué the peas. Next, appliqué each pod side and add the leafy top. If the top has too many deep curves, soften them to make appliqué easier.

However, there is another pod option if a single color of fabric is used (as in the more traditional quilt; see photo I-2). This method creates a gathered look along the inside edge of the pod. First, cut the pod in a "V" shape leaving the point connected.

Place it in its location on the background block, wrong side up, after cutting away the interior on the inside solid lines. Sew a running stitch where the dash lines occur. Place the interior pod fabric with the Master Pattern marked on it and baste it over the pod fabric, catching the inner seam allowance of the "V."

Stitch the peas in place. Give your imagination free rein when choosing fabrics. Fabrics with circles or designs can be fussy-cut to position light and dark shading, as in the sample, but other patterns are equally as effective.

Machine stitching options are also possible. Outline the peas with a satin stitch or top stitch them. The example is hand appliquéd. Though the design gives the impression the peas are full circles, in reality only the top and bottom edges are appliquéd. The sides are just attached with a running stitch. Trim the curves to a scant 1/8" to have them roll smoothly. A small amount of stuffing can be added to provide extra loft. Too much will cause the background block to stretch out of shape.

Not sure if you want to stuff the peas? Stitch the entire pod and then decide. Stuffing is added by cutting a small slit in the background fabric under the pea. Stuff and whipstitch the backing closed, but do not pull the edges of the fabric together. That will make the fabric warp out of shape. Stuffing will not be very obvious until it is outline quilted, then the pea will pop forward.

Photo 11-4
Basting of the pod and the inner shell with Master Pattern lines for the pea appliqué. Markings on the template serve dual purposes.

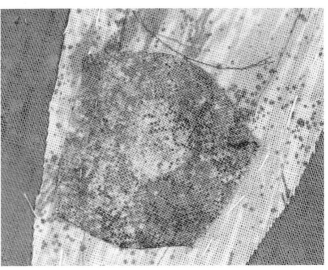

Photo 11-5
Only the top and bottom curves are appliquéd. Each side is held in place with running stitches.

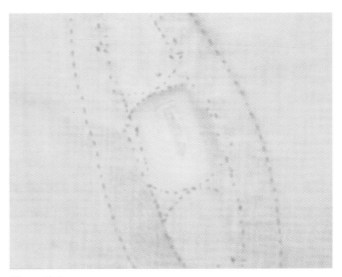

Photo 11-6
Stuffing the pea through the backing requires that the slit be closed with large whipstitches. Do not pull the edges together or it will warp.

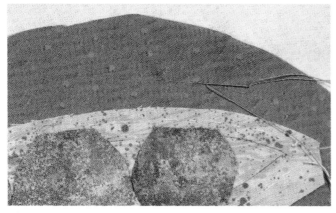

Photo 11-7
Stitch to the Master Pattern of the pod's outer edge with a running stitch.

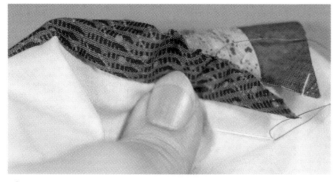

Photo 11-8
Push in the pod fabric, fold under the seam, and stitch the excess in place.

Photo 11-9
Fold the end of the point into the pod. Trim as necessary and stitch to the point.

Photo 11-10
Fold the remaining side in; trim. Fold and stitch.

Attach the outer edges of the pod to the Master Pattern laid on the background block with running stitches.

Start at the stem end and push the pod fabric over to the stitching line on the pod's inside.

Notice that there is excess fabric. Finger-press it directly toward the pencil line. Do not push it at an angle or the excess fabric cannot be worked in. As you stitch, trim the seam allowance as necessary to about 1/8". Stitches placed close together will hold down the excess.

Continue appliquéing down the entire edge to just before the point. Trim the point to a scant 1/4", and fold it back toward the pod. Continue stitching right to the point.

Trim the seam allowance as necessary, and fold in the unstitched side overlapping the point. Sew back up the remaining side. Appliqué the leafy top.

Vines

Applying a narrow strip of fabric is accomplished as detailed in Chapter 3: Narrow Stems (see page 42). Now, there is an added challenge—curves. There are two issues to remember: The fabric must be cut on the bias, and always sew the inside curve first. This means that you will jump stitching from one side to another as the vine edge changes from an inside to outside curve.

A stem begins in a seam allowance area or where another appliqué will cover it. Sew to the pencil line on the inner curve side of the stem with a small running stitch. Keep its seam allowance within the two pencil lines. Maintain the same amount of seam allowance as the

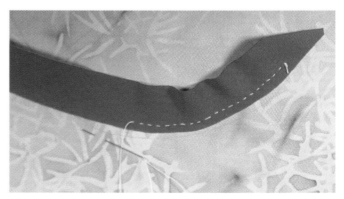

Photo 11-11
The inner side of the stem is attached with a running stitch. The seam allowance's edge is ruffled before appliquéing.

inner curve is stitched, using the needle's tip to manipulate the fabric around the curve. The seam allowance on the unstitched edge will be ruffled. Continue attaching the fabric until the pencil line turns and it becomes an outside curve. End the thread.

Push the fabric over into place and trim off the excess seam allowance. Turn it under and pin on the outside curve, trimming as necessary. Begin the appliqué stitching about 1/2" beyond the ending knot. Sew the outer curve in place back to where you began attaching the vine. Do make sure that the fabric is pushed straight over and is not at an angle, which will cause bias ripples. One portion of the vine is now complete.

Now, return to the unstitched end of the bias strip and tug gently to expose the first few appliqué stitches. This part is awkward. Begin the running stitch on the inner curve and continue on that side until a section is reached where it becomes an outer curve. Make sure that the running stitch is not gathered. See photo 11-14.

It is important to trim the seam allowance and clip almost to the stitching line on the outer curve. Hold your thumbnail directly on the pencil line; the seam allowance will curl back over your nail and it is easy to see how much to trim and how deep to clip. Continue appliquéing as explained above.

Note: When the inner curve is very acute, only two or three running stitches can be taken onto the needle.

Why is it necessary to stitch the inner curve first? Try sewing an outer curve first, then the inner curve. It is almost impossible to work in the excess fabric. By first stitching the inner curve, when the fabric is rolled over to the outer curve, the bias fabric expands to fit the larger distance. The result is a smooth, ripple-free vine.

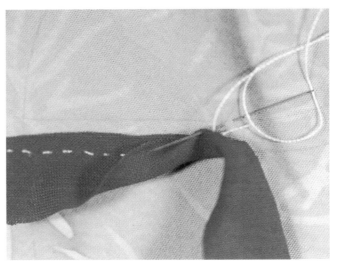

Photo 11-12
Trim and roll the fabric over to the outer curve. Turn under the seam allowance and stitch in place almost up to where the curve switches direction.

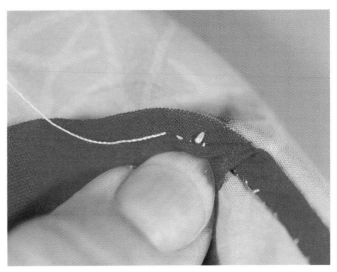

Photo 11-13
Go back to the inner curve (running stitch), start a new thread and continue the running stitch into the next outer curve.

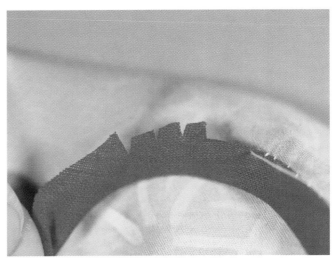

Photo 11-14
On the outer curve, clip almost to the stitching line.

Points to Remember:

❖ Trim close to the stitching line and clip almost to the seam line a scant 1/8" apart.

❖ Sew with short lengths of fabric, only going from one design area to another. Do not carry the vine under an area that will be covered with appliqué.

❖ Slight cupping that might occur within a loop will be removed with gentle pressing and quilting.

❖ Vines can also be machine satin stitched—just be sure to use a stabilizer.

The Dragonfly

This delightful insect is a favorite of many. It lends itself to a variety of fabric patterns and colors. Think iridescent, think transparent, or picture the myriad options of fabric designs that can depict wings. Also, consider machine embroidery options for the veining of the wings. For a wall quilt, sheer fabrics are a perfect choice, especially those that glimmer.

Photo 11-15
Dragonfly stitch with metallic wing fabric and thread.

Lightweight fabrics are not a good choice for a bed quilt, as the fabric will not last. This is the perfect place to emphasize the wings' transparency with metallic fabrics and decorative threads.

Assuming the pattern is already laid on the background block, begin with the dragonfly's wings. They can be sewn with machine satin stitch, buttonholed, or basic needleturn appliqué. Another option is to quilt following the fabric's design, as in the **What a Garden!** dragonfly. See photo 11-1.

Place a stabilizer under the background block and lay the wings in place. Using a decorative thread, straight stitch around the outside of each wing about 1/16" from the cut edge. The thread does not have to be ended between wings. Stitch one top wing, cross the center, and stitch around the opposite top wing, then cross the center again and stitch around both bottom wings in the same manner. Change to the decorative stitch of your choice and stitch around the wings as just described. Be sure that the straight stitching is covered, and have the decorative stitch just off the wing into the background block. Stitch the long tail in the same manner and repeat for the body, then the head.

ADDITIONAL THOUGHTS

There are a variety of items you can make from portions of the pea pod pattern. The dragonfly lends itself to clothing embellishment, pillows, or a single quilt block. I picture a quilt of dragonflies created using brilliant fabrics and decorative threads. To see photographs of dragonflies, search the Internet by typing *dragonfly* in the Search text box. The South American varieties are especially vibrant.

The next chapter details how to assemble all the blocks together into the completed top and how to prepare and turn the fabric sandwich into a completed quilt.

chapter 12

Assembling the Top

THE TOP'S ASSEMBLY

Stitching is completed, and it is time to see how the blocks look assembled into the completed top. If the blocks are wrinkled, this is the time for a final pressing. Be careful: Pressing is not ironing. Accurate work is undone with a too-enthusiastic application of a hot iron.

Using the schematic of the quilt design (illus. 2-1), lay the quilt blocks out in order of assembly. Begin working in rows across the top of the quilt. The piecing can either be by hand or machine. Both examples are machine pieced with 1/4" seams.

Borders

Follow the schematic in illus. 2-1 to hand or machine piece the bricks around the border. They are the same *cut size* (2-1/2" x 4") as those used in both brick blocks. Notice in the schematic that there are partial bricks near the corners. Piece the inner row first, one side at a

Backing Yardage

4 yds, approximately, based on 44" wide fabric, sewn together on the horizontal. Yardage will vary depending on the top's finished size.

Row One: Join the pear on its right side to the leaf bricks. Next add the flowers times two.
Row Two: Join asparagus on its right side to the onion. Next add the flower. Do not add the peas at this time.
The next two rows are joined as a unit.
Rows Three/Four: Join the pots to daisy/fence and add peppers along its bottom edge. Finally, add the snail bricks.
Join Rows One/Two to Rows Three/Four
Finally, complete the top by setting in the pea pods.

time, then add the outer row in the same manner. This makes it easier to figure how many partial bricks are needed and where they should be inserted. It is best not to set them as the last ones at the corner. Rather, piece them in the row one or two blocks before the corners.

There is another option. An 8"-wide border of fencing would create a delightful enclosure for your **Savory Garden**. Make two paper Master Patterns one-half the length and width of the quilt's interior. Trace the fence pattern onto each, adjusting the spacing between the rails so that they balance around the corners. Appliqué the fence and join to quilt's interior.

Preparing the Top

There are two final steps before assembling the quilt with batting and backing. First, check to make sure all wrinkles are removed. Second, clip off loose threads hanging from the seam allowances. It is tedious and time-consuming, but necessary—why? Once the top is assembled, and especially after quilting, loose threads can become visible from the right side of the quilt, particularly if a light background was used.

Preparing the Backing

Backing fabric can be plain or printed. If the punch and poke stitch is used or you are a new quilter, I recommend a print fabric and quilt thread color that blends with it so any imperfect quilting stitches on the quilt's back are not obvious.

CAUTION:
When clipping raveling threads, use care not to cut the top. It has happened.

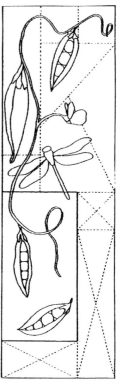

Illus. 12-1
Schematic of the quilt top assembly.

Measure the top. Cut the backing 4" larger on all sides. There are two good reasons for this:

1. The excess backing is basted over the batting to protect it from snagging during quilting.
2. When quilting the edge, the basting is removed, and the extra backing fabric is clamped in the hoop to provide adequate tension along the quilt's edge.

Choosing a Batting for a Specific Look

❖ "What batting do I use?" and "Which will be best for my top?" With the proliferation of quilt battings on the market, these are the two most frequently asked questions. My answer is short. "It depends":

❖ What do you want the quilt to look like after the quilting is finished? Old fashioned? More modern? Flat, or with higher loft between the rows of quilting?

- ❖ How warm do you want it to be?
- ❖ Is it to be machine or hand quilted?
- ❖ If hand quilted, what type of quilting stitch do you use? Running, or punch and poke?
- ❖ Do you use a thimble?
- ❖ How far apart will the quilting rows be placed?
- ❖ How much time do you have to get it quilted?

The answer to the "What batting do I use?" question is determined by the sum of all your responses. There is no right or wrong choice, and batting selection may change from quilt to quilt. Here is information to help with your answers:

- ❖ Using a cotton batting creates an "old quilt" appearance.

- ❖ Polyester batting usually produces a higher loft between the rows of quilting, resulting in a more modern appearance.

- ❖ Polyester batting is usually warmer than cotton batting. Wool is also warm.

- ❖ There is no difference between machine quilting with cotton or polyester.

- ❖ Running stitch quilting is difficult, or impossible, using a thick batting.

- ❖ Punch and poke quilting can be done on either a thick or thin batting, no matter the fiber content.

- ❖ A thimble should be used for the running stitch. It is not required for the punch and poke stitch.

- ❖ Read the batting's packaging recommendations for distance between the quilt rows. If cotton has scrim (stabilizing film) or is needlepunched to hold the fibers together, it can be quilted 4" to 6" apart. The same applies to polyester.

- ❖ Cotton batting with non-stabilized fibers may move after washing or with frequent use. Quilt 1" to 2" apart to keep it from shifting.

- ❖ Polyester batting that is bonded in some fashion can be quilted 6" apart.

There is one caveat that should influence your decision and pertains to both cotton and polyester: Fiber migration through the quilt to the surface. It happens less often with cotton, so the focus will be on polyester. When polyester batting first came on the market there was a major migrating problem. Frequently a quilt with unbonded polyester looked like it needed a surface shave—not a good thing! Happily, bonding addressed that problem. Before choosing a brand, however, ask a quilt shop owner or quilter for the latest information about migrating fibers.

Basting the Top, Batting, and Backing

Cut off the selvedges, sew the backing together into a single piece, and press the seam open. The result is a backing 72" x 88". The following directions are for hand basting, which is my favored method. Yes, there are other methods, but this always produces a quilt that is straight and does not shift.

1. Give the back of the top a final haircut! Trim off all loose threads.
2. Lay the backing onto a carpet, wrong side up. Pin the backing to the carpet, squaring it up with a wall. First, pin along one side, then the opposite side, pulling slightly to bring the fabric under slight tension and remove wrinkles. Pin the third side, and finally, the fourth side, again pulling gently. The entire quilt backing is squared and basted to the floor, under slight tension.
3. Float the batting onto the backing, centering it. Gently remove all wrinkles. Do not pin the batting.
4. Center the top, right side up, over the batting. Make sure it is squared with the sides of the backing that extend beyond the batting.
5. Repeat the pinning process, using the same pins that hold the backing in place. The two fabrics are now pinned into the carpet with the batting sandwiched in between. Baste the fabric sandwich together using basting thread. Basting thread is a white thread that breaks easily, and is removed after the quilting is completed. There is no logical reason to baste diagonally. Straight serpentine basting rows about 4" apart

Illus. 12-2
Serpentine basting rows are 4" apart. The basting holds the "sandwich" together during quilting.

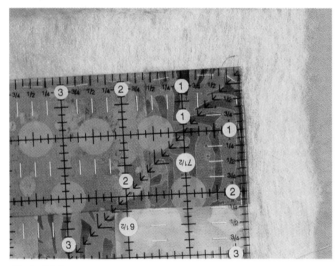

Photo 12-1
The quilt's corner is square with a ruler.

CAUTION:

To prevent unnecessary stretching, never leave the quilt in any hoop—even when putting it down for ten minutes. When placing the quilt in the hoop, always open it up wider than necessary. Push the hoop ring together with your hands and clamp it tight. Quilting is not like embroidery that is worked drum tight.

hold everything together. In my experience, shifting has never occurred. Begin at one short end and pull the pins out as you baste across the end. Baste up the side 4", and begin another row of basting back across the quilt. As the pins are removed, the quilt can be rolled up. Continue until the entire unit is basted and all the pins are removed.

6. Double check that the corners are square. Once the basting is completed, fold the excess backing fabric over the quilt's raw edges, encasing the batting. Baste it in the outer seam allowance.

Deciding on a Quilt Design

The choice of a quilting pattern affects the look of your quilt. In pictorial designs such as the **Savory Garden**, it is best to outline quilt the shapes to make them pop forward. The traditional example (photo I-2) was quilted on a long-arm machine. The background was stipple quilted. The **What A Garden!** quilt is hand quilted. Each block is quilted within the design and the shape outline quilted. Sometimes the fabric design was followed, other times not. The background was echo quilted about 1" apart, but could be crosshatched with 1" lines. The option is yours.

Photo 12-2
Close-up of the daisy and surrounding areas

Choosing the Right Hoop

The selection of a quilt hoop is very personal. There are large and mid-sized floor frames, portable frames, stands with hoops attached, and unattached hoops made from wood and plastic in varying shapes. Selection depends on what type of chair you sit in, room temperature (sweating can become an art form in summer), portability, your back, and the type of quilting stitch. The best hoop is one that works for you.

After trying many styles, I now use a 12" plastic quilting hoop. Here is my reasoning: I sit on the couch with one leg crossed over the other to quilt. A 12" hoop does not slip off my knee, as larger ones do. The quilt is bunched up on the hoop's far edge to support the weight, leaving both my hands free. Plastic does not transfer wood oil marks on the fabric.

The Quilting Stitch

Numerous books discuss the running stitch, but almost none address a feasible option: Punch and poke quilting. Therefore, this section deals only with the latter—and my brief story.

I began quilting in 1975, and the running stitch was not for me, since I do not use a thimble. With a background in needlepoint and cross-stitch, using two hands to work the needle was natural, so I tried it with quilting. It worked.

Yes, it takes time to learn, but so does the running stitch. Yes, it takes longer to quilt this way, but speed is not my motivation—accuracy is. I want the same length stitches and spaces on the top and on the backing. The running stitch physics of a needle moving diagonally through three layers of fabric, catching the backing and coming back up almost always produces tiny stitches and larger spaces on the back—the opposite from the front. Not so with punch and poke. After some practice, stitch and space length will be the same on both the top and back … and you'll have no pricked fingers.

The major advantage for many quilters is that punch and poke requires little hand pres-

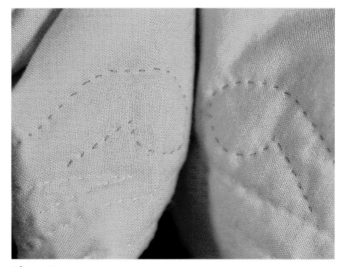

Photo 12-3
Comparison of top and backing stitches. Can you tell which is which? The top is on the right.

sure. Rejoice all quilters with arthritis or carpel tunnel syndrome! You can quilt.

Beginning a Quilt Thread without a Knot

First, a word about thread color. It can coordinate with your background fabric and blend with the appliqué, or stand out. There is no hard and fast rule. Your quilting stitches might be the deciding factor. Do you want them to be obvious or blend into the fabrics? The **What a Garden!** quilt used ten colors, but the traditional has only two—off-white and tan.

Quilting requires a Between or quilting needle and quilt thread. Refer back to the Introduction: Quilting Basics, Thread (page 10), for a review. Quilting frays thread, so a working thread should be no longer than 15", but cut a length double what is needed—no more than 30". Rub it with a coating compound and thread the needle. Bring the needle to the center of the thread.

The quilt is now in a hoop or frame. It does not matter which hand stays on top and which works under the frame; determine which to use after trying both. Punch the needle into the quilt at the starting point and bring the needle to the back. Pull one-half the thread through. There is 15" on top and 15" under the quilt. Return the needle to the surface, and pull the 15" up and slip the needle to its center. You are ready to quilt with one 15" length.

Photo 12-4
Punch the needle into the fabric absolutely vertical to the top. Do not put the needle in at an angle and tip it upright; doing so creates diagonal stitches.

Use the index finger as a "pusher," rather like a plunger. With the needle held between thumb and middle finger, punch the needle vertically down into the top.

Spread your fingers and push up slightly on the backing. Receive the needle as it comes through.

Pull the needle through with the hand underneath the quilt, just enough to turn the needle around; do not pull the thread all the way through to the back because it takes your hand away from the spot where the needle must be returned to the surface.

Repeat the punch and poke stitch. Punch it down, turn the needle around, poke it back up, and pull the thread taut, one stitch at a time.

Photo 12-5
Hold your fingers spread out and receive the needle as it comes through to the back.

Photo 12-6
Pull the thread through, only enough to turn it around and poke it back to the surface.

Photo 12-7
Pull each thread tight after the needle returns to the surface. Taking two or three stitches before pulling the thread creates uneven tension.

That's it, but perhaps your stitches are angled, especially on the back. What went wrong? This stitch requires holding the needle in a different way. For your entire quilting life, the needle has been held at a horizontal angle for appliqué, piecing, and running stitch quilting. The punch and poke stitch requires retraining your fingers to hold the needle like a plunger between thumb and middle finger. There must be no fudging or there will be angled stitches.

Study photo 12-9. Novices poke the needle in at an angle, tip the needle upright, and punch it through. Wrong! Quilting this way makes angled stitches. Retrain your fingers to hold the needle so it goes into the fabric absolutely straight. This technique pertains to the underside also.

Most punch and poke stitches look good on the top from the start. The underside's angled stitches require time to perfect. Expect to finish a small project before you are happy with the quilting stitches on the back. For this reason, I suggest that a quilter who is new to the punch and poke technique use a print fabric for the backing and a color thread that blends into it. This way, the stitches look terrific on the top and any less-than-perfect stitches on the underside are not obvious. Once backing stitches are straight, go for it: Use solid color fabrics and contrasting thread, then show both sides with a confidant smile.

Is it worth spending time retraining your hands? My students certainly think so, and their quilted projects prove it. Perfecting the running stitch also takes time. The stitches and spaces on the back are rarely the same size as on the top however many projects are completed. Even so, there are more reasons to use the punch and poke stitch.

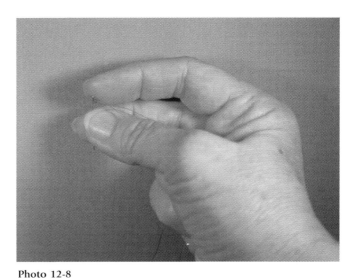

Photo 12-8
Retrain your fingers to hold the needle between thumb and middle finger like a plunger.

Photo 12-9
Punch the needle into the top. Let go and see if it remains vertical. If not, remove and try again.

Circles—try them with the running stitch! The running stitch does not work to make circles. Right handed running stitch quilters can quilt angles from right to left, but not in a left to right direction. When you use the punch and poke method, a frame does not have to be turned. You can quilt in all directions, up or down, left to right and right to left, and thus: Circles!

IMPORTANT!
Once the needle is brought to the quilt's surface, always pull the thread through after each stitch. Do not take several stitches and then pull the thread taut. This will cause uneven tension and make the quilt pucker.

Photo 12-10
The snail quilted on the top without rotating the hoop. Circles!

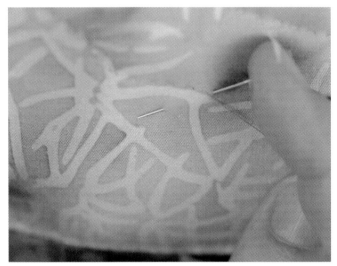

Photo 12-11
To end, pull on the thread and poke the needle into the hole where the thread comes out. Take the needle through the batting and bring it out to the surface. Pull until the loop disappears. (See photos 12-13).

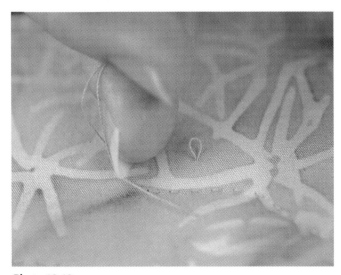

Photo 12-12
Repeat this above step two more times, always going in a different direction and crossing a line of quilting. The loop is left for demonstration.

However, expertise with the poke and punch method does not develop overnight. I first worked right to left, always turning the hoop until the stitches were good, on both front and back. Next, I perfected quilting down-up and up-down. Soon I could go in any direction with equal results.

There is a crutch that helps when first learning punch and poke quilting. Place two pins on either side of the quilting line about 1" apart—doing so helps compress the fabric. This trick also works for running-stitch quilters. Move the pins as the quilting progresses. Soon you will be quilting, forget to move the pins and discover they are not necessary anymore.

Moving Thread between Design Areas

What if you reach the end of a design shape and still have thread left? It is easy to move from one area to another by running the needle through the batting from one spot to another. Just do not move it more than an inch or so. In that instance, end the thread and thread the other end of the quilting length—you started in its middle, after all—and go to the next area.

Ending a Quilt Thread without a Knot

Ending the thread tail is easy and it is more secure than a knot—promise. At the end of a design pattern or where outline quilting is completed, make the last stitch a backstitch into the batting. Do not go through to the backing.

Bring the thread length all the way through to the surface. Pull gently on the thread and put the needle's tip into the hole where the thread comes out. Run the needle through the batting in a different direction, crossing a line of quilting and bring the needle back up to the surface. Tug on the thread until the thread loop drops into the batting. Repeat two more times, always going in a different direction and crossing a quilt line, if possible. Cut off the thread tail. The thread is woven into the batting and locked in. No knots popping to the surface—and the thread is absolutely secure.

Joining Quilt Stitches

Once the thread is ended, place the needle on the unused tail and begin quilting with it. When reaching a place where two quilting lines meet, the joining stitch must be repeated in the following manner or a stitch will be skipped on the quilt's back: Come up through the hole of the joining stitch and back down into its far side. Run the needle through the batting and bring it to the surface a short distance away. Repeat the weaving process into the batting as detailed above, or run the thread through the batting to another area.

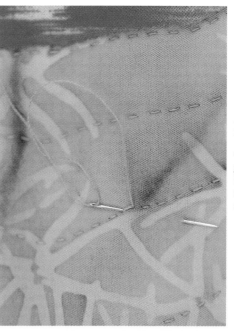

Photo 12-13
When a row of stitches meets, the joining stitch must be repeated or a stitch on the backing will be skipped.

Quilting along the Quilt's Edge

Each of the border bricks must be quilted along its outer edge. It is hard to gauge this line before the binding is applied. This outer quilting row is best left until after the binding is attached to the quilt, but before it is rolled over the edge to encase the quilt's raw edge. Quilt to within 1" of the quilt's edge. Pull the needle off and let the threads dangle until the binding is attached with a 1/4" seam. See page 114, Binding the Quilt, for the remaining steps.

Photo 12-14
Hooped after the binding is machine sewn to the front, the thread dangles loose, ready for quilting.

Checking Quilt Thread Tension

The fabric sandwich must be held together with a quilting stitch of correct tension: Firm (short of puckering), yet not too loose. Too tight is easy to check. Is the fabric sandwich puckered? Do not tug on the quilting thread so hard when pulling the thread through after each stitch. Too loose may not be as apparent. In the middle of a quilted row, slip the needle's tip under a stitch and pull up. There should be no excess. If a loop forms, correct the tension by pulling the thread more taut.

Hints to Perfect the Quilting Stitch

❖ Keep one hand under the quilt and the other on top. *Don't cheat!* Moving one hand to turn the needle on the underside and bringing the same hand back to the top will take forever.

❖ Use the proper needle and thread: A Between and quilt thread. Never use a Sharp or regular sewing thread.

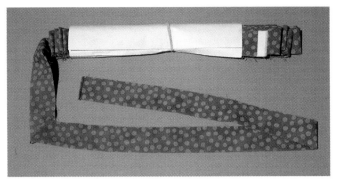

Photo 12-15
Piece the entire binding together, press in half and fan fold, then place into a tube for easy control.

Photo 12-16
Sew the binding to the front through all layers and trim the batting and backing to 1/2".

Machine Quilting

Many quilters prefer to use a home sewing machine or a long-arm quilting machine to attach the three layers together. Machine quilting is certainly faster, but it does not provide the same finished appearance as does hand quilting—not a bad thing, just different. Here are some suggestions that help with home sewing machine quilting.

❖ Wear cloth gloves with gripper dots on the palm and fingers to help control the basted quilt when free-motion quilting.

❖ Drop the feed dogs for free motion quilting and use a darning foot. The stitch length is determined by how fast you move the fabric sandwich. Use a needle-down position if available.

❖ Quilting can be done with the feed dogs in place and a regular foot. The advantage is an equal length stitch length, but it is more difficult to turn the fabric. Use a needle-down position if available.

❖ Basting is important. Many quilters prefer safety pin basting. I prefer basting thread.

❖ Use an ironing board alongside the sewing machine to help support the quilt's weight.

Trimming the Quilt

The **Savory Garden** quilt does not require mitered corners or bias binding because the borders are not mitered and the quilt edges are straight. Cut seven 2-1/2"-wide strips across the width of the fabric. Machine sew them together. Use a straight seam; a mitered edge is not necessary. Press the seams open. Fold the strip in half, wrong sides together. Press. Fan-fold the long strip. Seal an envelope and cut off both ends. Slip the fan-folded binding into the envelope and fold the excess paper over to make a neat tube. Hold it together with a rubber band. The binding is now controlled for easy use.

Binding the Quilt

Binding can be applied by hand, machine, or with a combination of both. It can be attached to the backing and rolled to the front, or sewn to the front and rolled to the backing— your choice. The example is machine stitched to the front, rolled to the backing, and hand stitched.

Before binding, the quilt's outer edges must be trimmed and the corners squared. Lay a ruler along the outer edge and trim off the excess, leaving a scant 1/2" so that the binding will be filled with batting. First, position a square ruler on top of the corners to confirm that the corners are square (photo 12-1). If measuring, cutting, and piecing were accurate, little or no trimming should be required. Trim away the excess batting and backing.

Begin on the long sides first. Take several measurements along the length of the quilt. Pick one and cut the two bindings to that length. Find the middle of the binding and the quilt's edge.

Position the binding along the 1/4" seam and pin it at the quilt's center and work out toward the ends. The ends will be flush with the border's edge. The quilt will probably have to be eased to fit the binding. This happens because the outer edges are not quilted yet and quilting always shrinks the fabric sandwich. Hand or machine stitch the binding to the quilt through all layers.

Measure the quilt's width, add 2", and cut the binding strips to length. Pin to the quilt's edges, leaving 1" extending at both ends. Stitch to the quilt and trim as before.

Now extend the binding and clamp it in the hoop (or your frame), using it as a tool to keep the quilt under tension while those dangling threads are quilted along the brick's outer edges. See photo 12-14. Finish quilting each of the brick's outer edges with the dangling threads the same distance away from the binding that is used throughout your quilt. The sample was quilted 1/8" from the seam, which is less common than the standard 1/4".

At both ends, fold over the excess fabric and pin it in place (see photo 12-17). The excess can be trimmed to about 1/4". Roll the binding over to encase the raw edges. Pin in place. The binding should roll to just outside the stitching line that attached the first side. Machine or hand blind-stitch in place. I prefer hand stitching, and use the same stitch used for appliqué (see Chapter 2: The Appliqué Stitch, page 30). Machine attachment is fine, but my problem is getting the stitching straight on the reverse side.

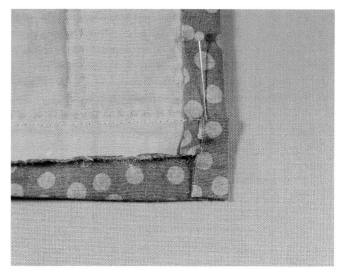

Photo 12-17
Fold in the end and trim to about 1/4" and pin in place.

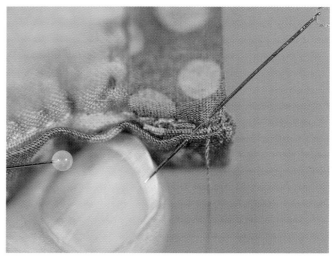

Photo 12-18
Roll over the binding to encase the raw edges. Whipstitch the binding so that all ends are encased within the binding.

Storing Quilts

❖ Never, never store quilts in a plastic bag. Quilts must breath or they will rot.

❖ Store quilts in an old, washed pillowcase, or make a bag using washed fabric.

❖ Refold quilts every six months to prevent permanent creases: Quarters one time, thirds the next.

❖ Use your quilts gently and your descendants will have an heirloom to treasure.

Photo 12-19
Backstitch your name and the date on the quilt top using quilting thread.

ADDITIONAL THOUGHTS

Your quilt is finished, but there are two more important things for you to do before doing the happy dance. Always backstitch your name and the completion date with quilting thread on the top and make a fabric label for the backing.

Include on the label the maker's name, date completed with the full year, why and for whom it was made, and any special story that you want to live along with the quilt. Use a permanent marker for writing. It helps to temporarily stabilize the fabric label for writing by ironing a piece of freezer paper on the reverse side. Stitch the label in a corner on the backing, and when the 22nd century rolls around, your descendants will thank you.

Now, dance away—your **Savory Garden** is complete!

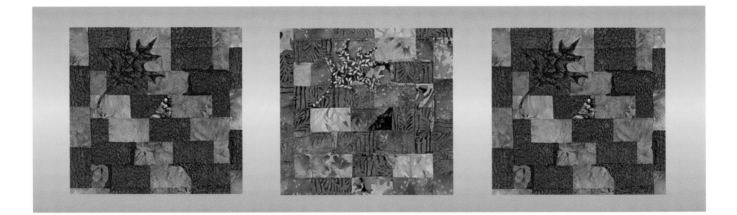

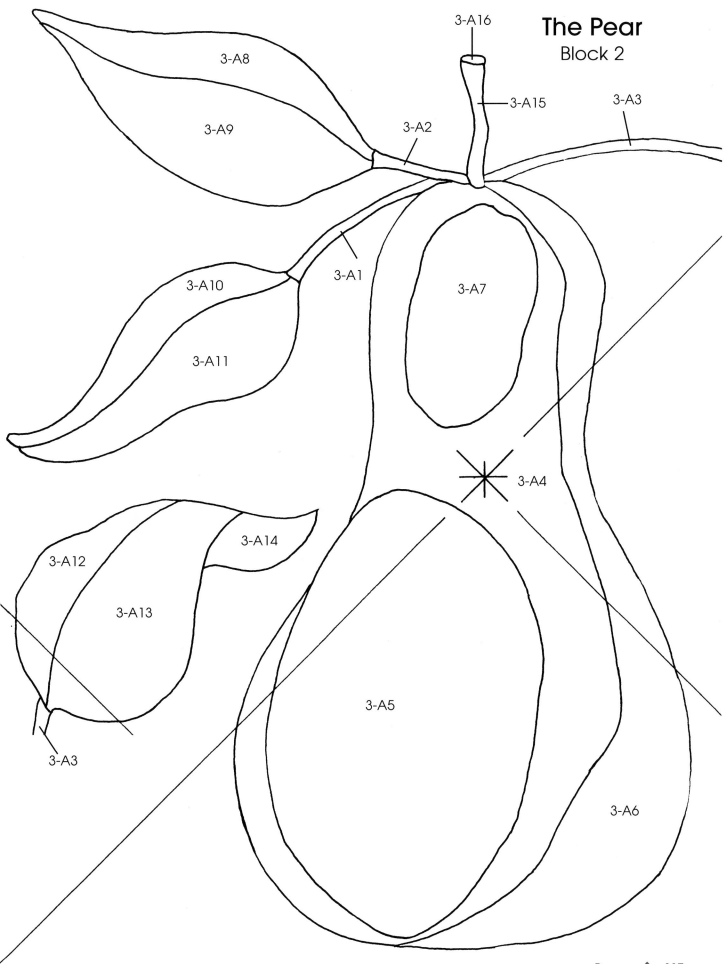

3-A16

The Pear
Block 2

3-A15

3-A3

3-A8

3-A9

3-A2

3-A1

3-A10

3-A7

3-A11

3-A4

3-A14

3-A12

3-A13

3-A5

3-A6

3-A3

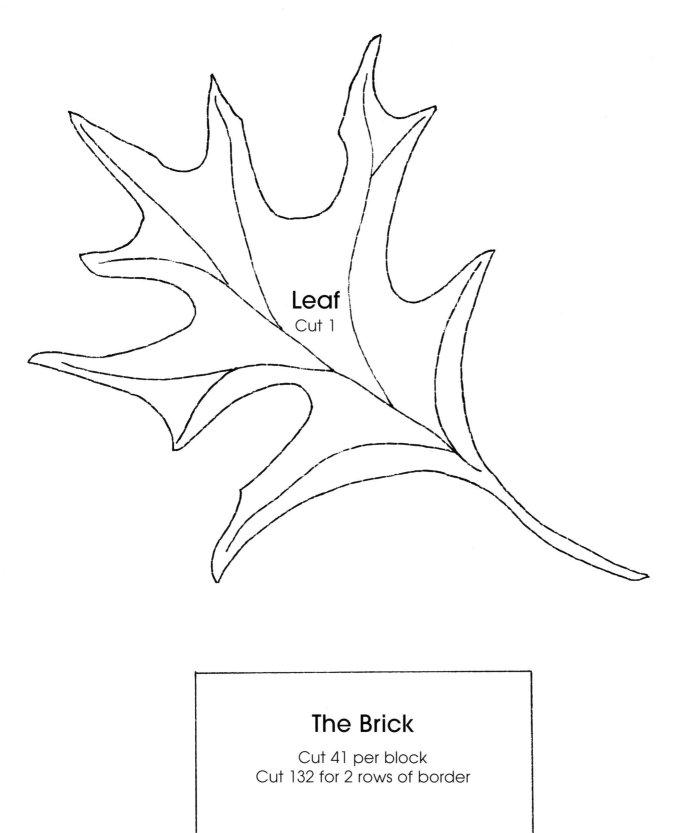

Leaf
Cut 1

The Brick

Cut 41 per block
Cut 132 for 2 rows of border

←——→

The Snail

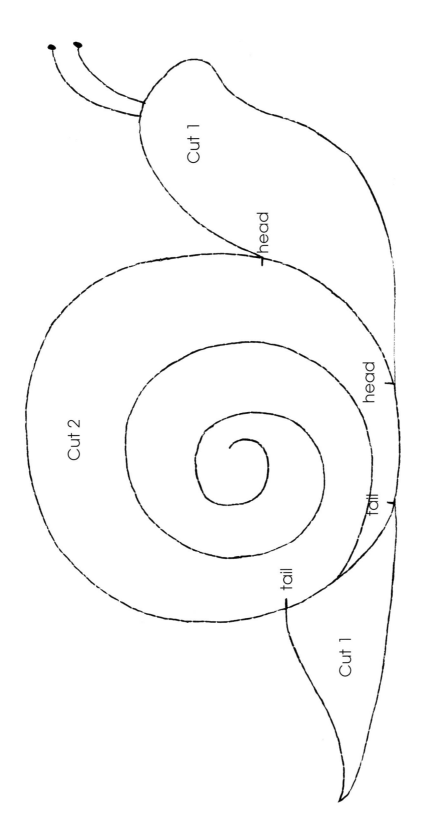

Cut 1

head

head

Cut 2

tail

tail

Cut 1

The Pots
Block 5

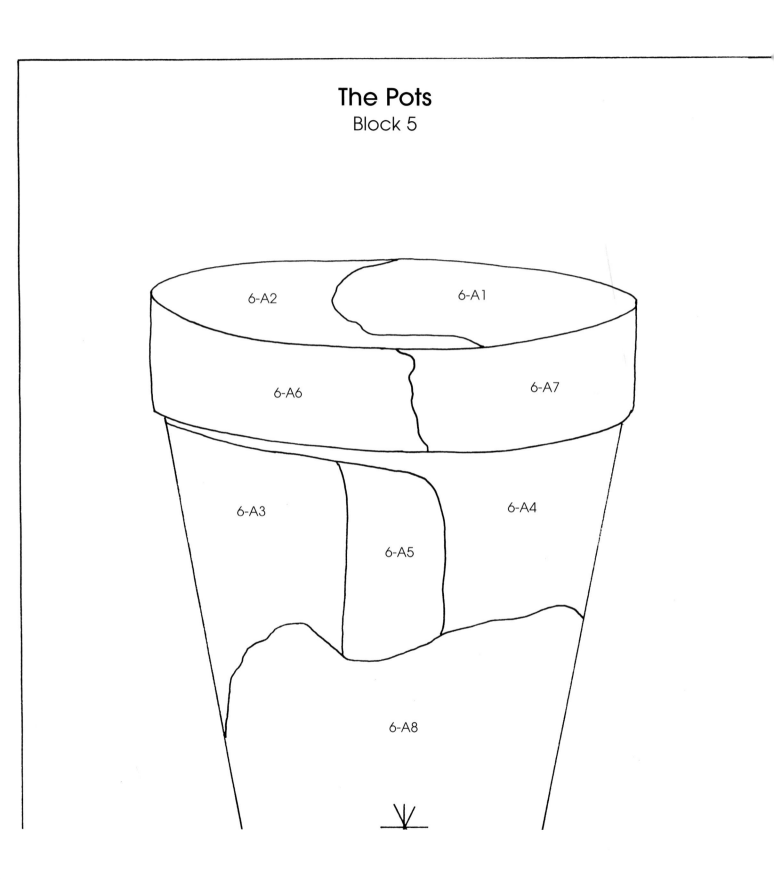

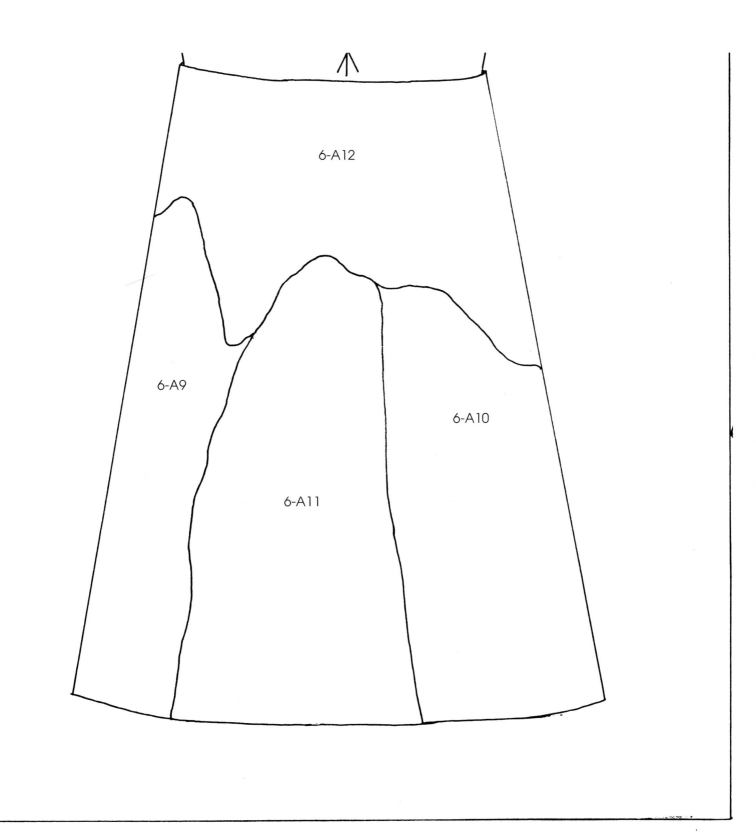

6-A12

6-A9

6-A10

6-A11

The Onion
Block 6

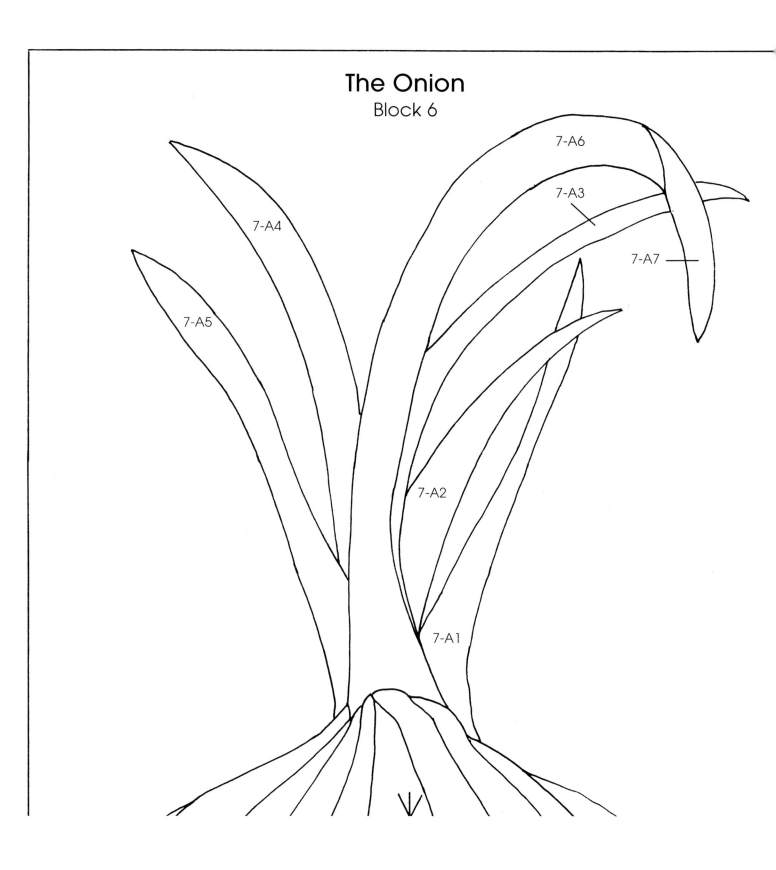

7-A6

7-A3

7-A4

7-A7

7-A5

7-A2

7-A1

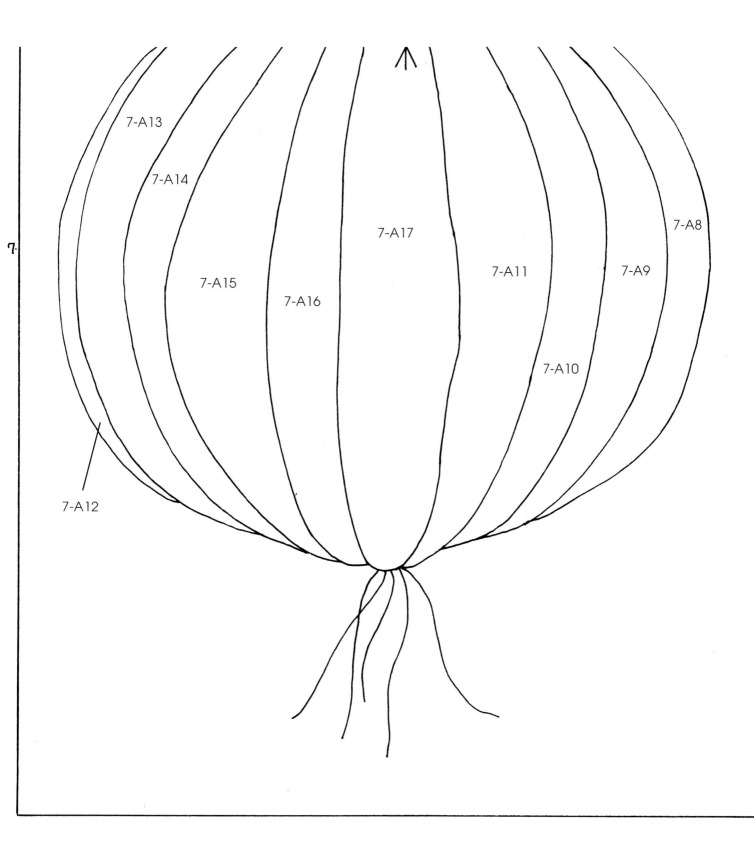

7-A13

7-A14

7-A17

7-A15

7-A16

7-A11

7-A9

7-A8

7-A10

7-A12

7·

Asparagus
Block 7

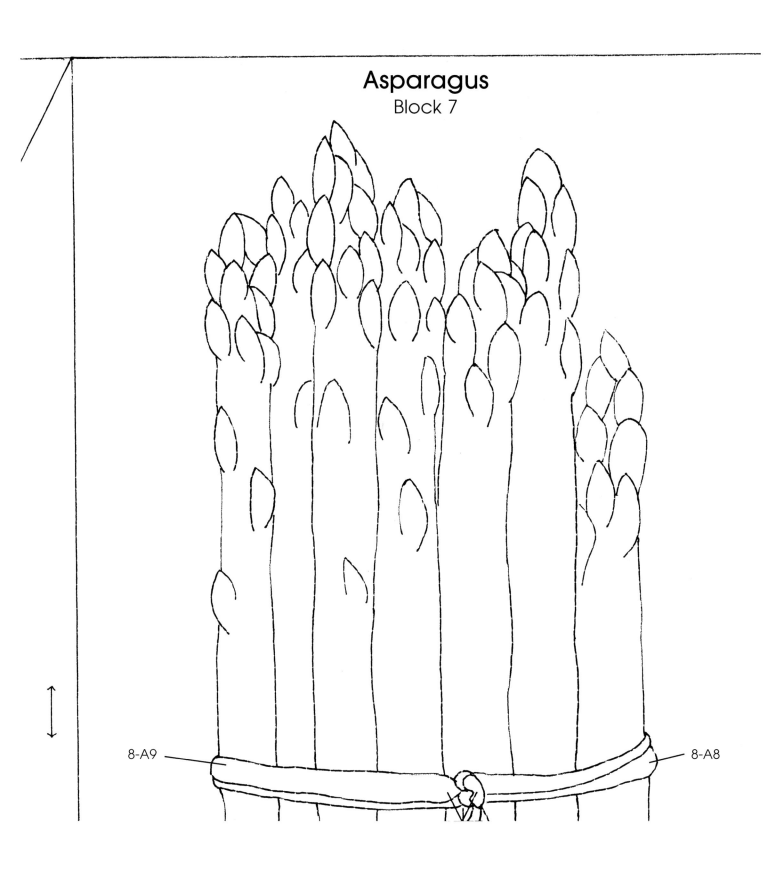

8-A9

8-A8

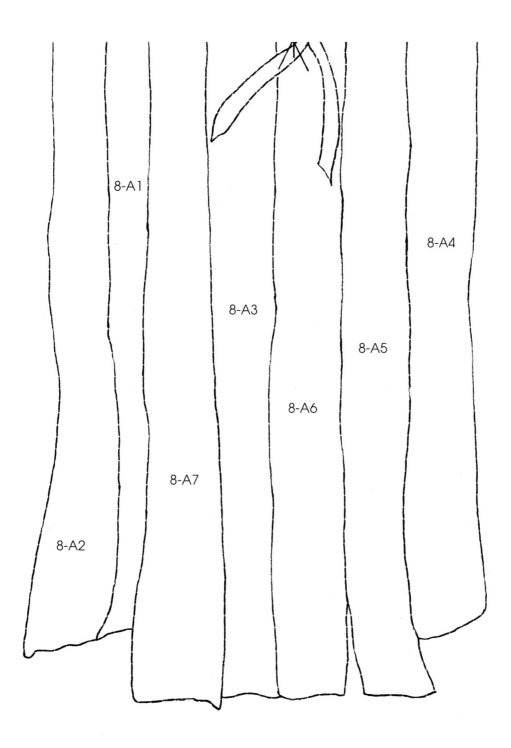

Peppers
Block 8

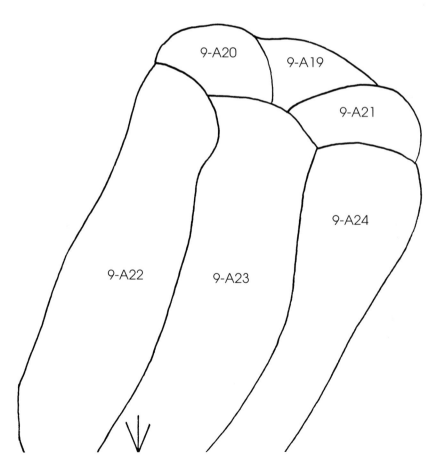

9-A28

9-A27

9-A29

9-A25

9-A26

9-A31

9-A33

9-A32

9-A30

9-A20

9-A19

9-A21

9-A24

9-A22

9-A23

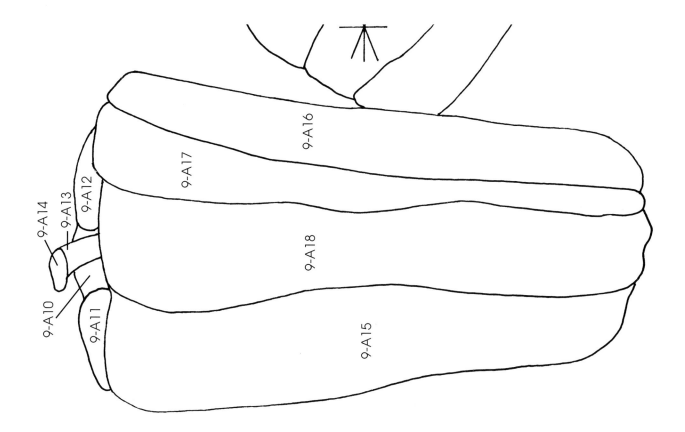

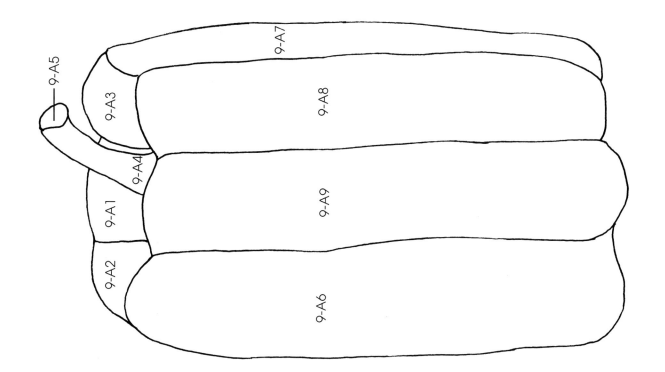

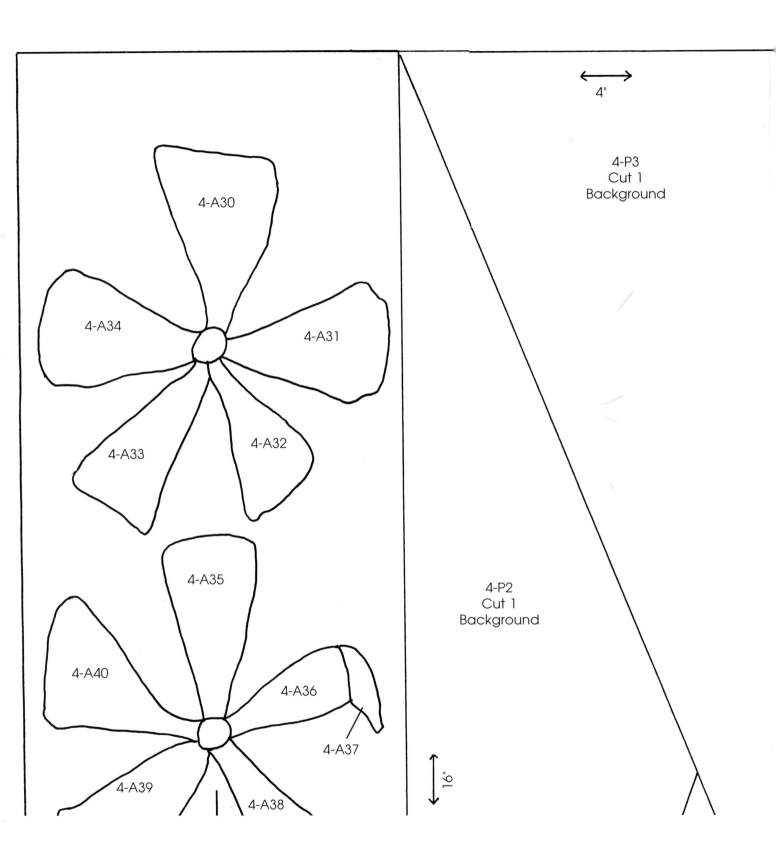

4"

4-P3
Cut 1
Background

4-A30

4-A34

4-A31

4-A33

4-A32

4-P2
Cut 1
Background

4-A35

4-A40

4-A36

4-A37

16"

4-A39

4-A38

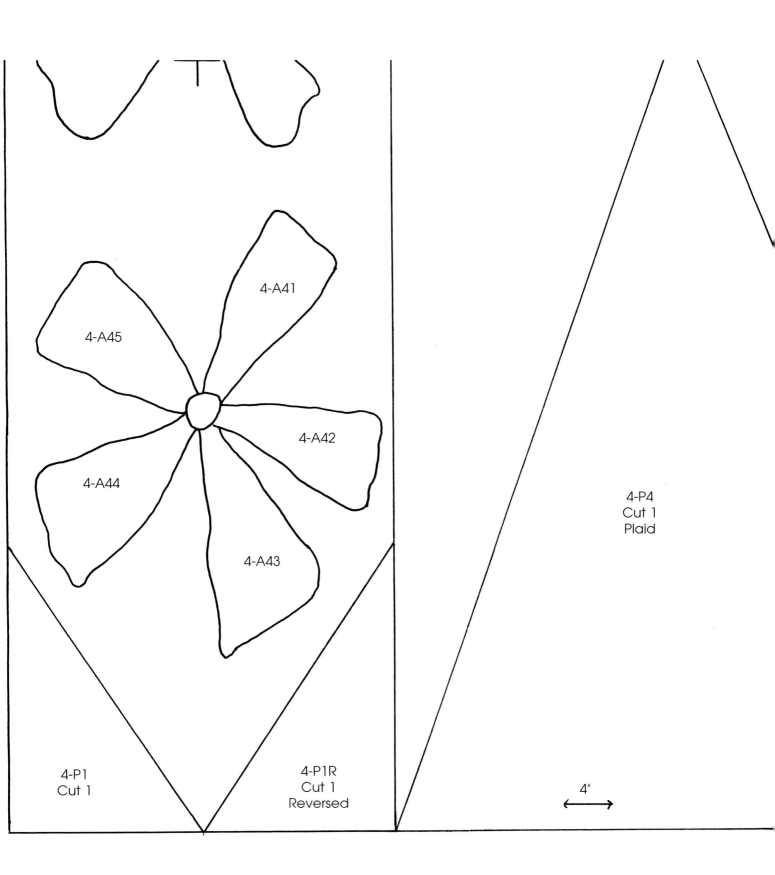

4-A41

4-A45

4-A42

4-A44

4-A43

4-P4
Cut 1
Plaid

4-P1
Cut 1

4-P1R
Cut 1
Reversed

4"

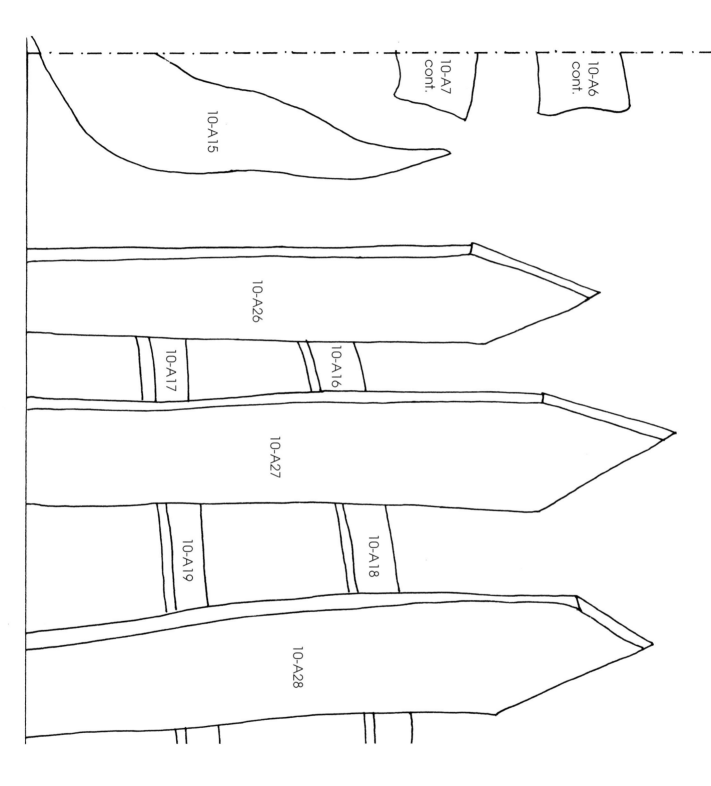

10-A7
cont.

10-A6
cont.

10-A15

10-A26

10-A17

10-A16

10-A27

10-A19

10-A18

10-A28

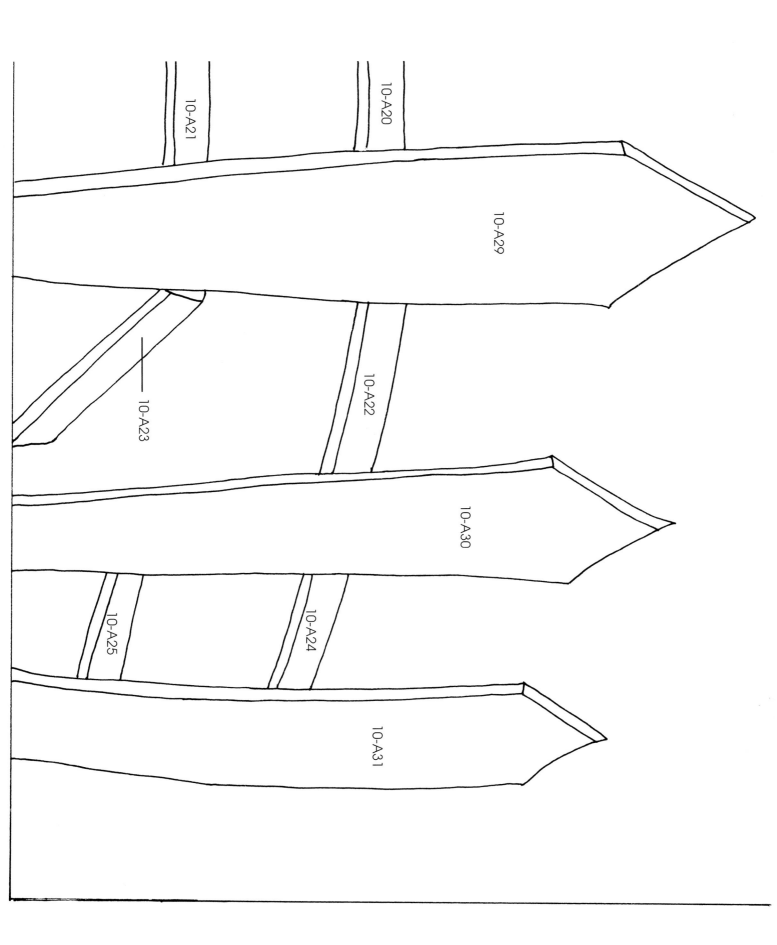

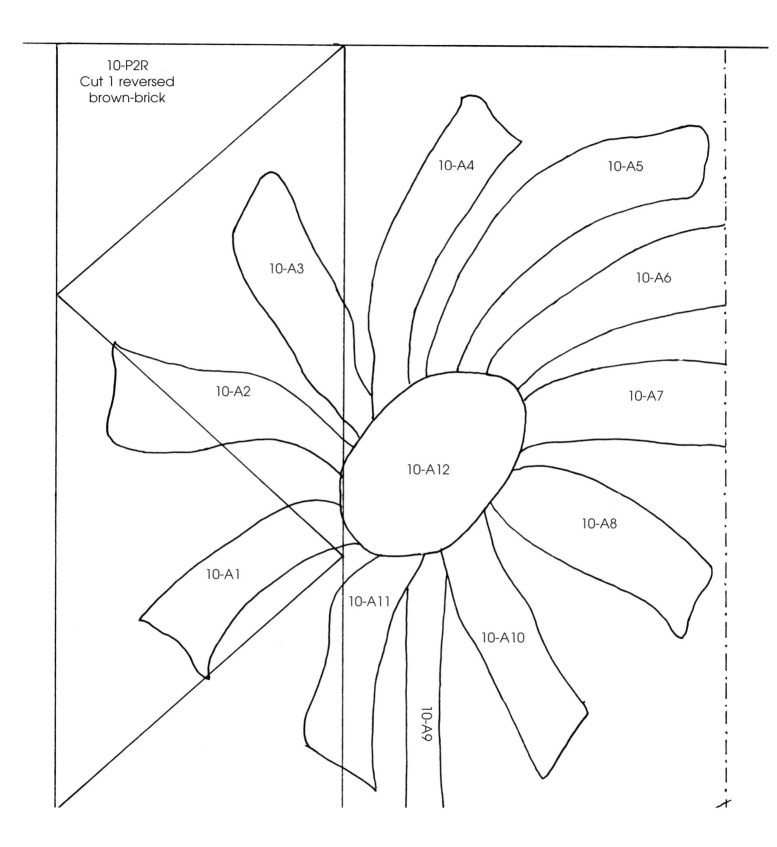

10-P2R
Cut 1 reversed
brown-brick

10-A4

10-A5

10-A3

10-A6

10-A2

10-A7

10-A12

10-A8

10-A1

10-A11

10-A10

10-A9

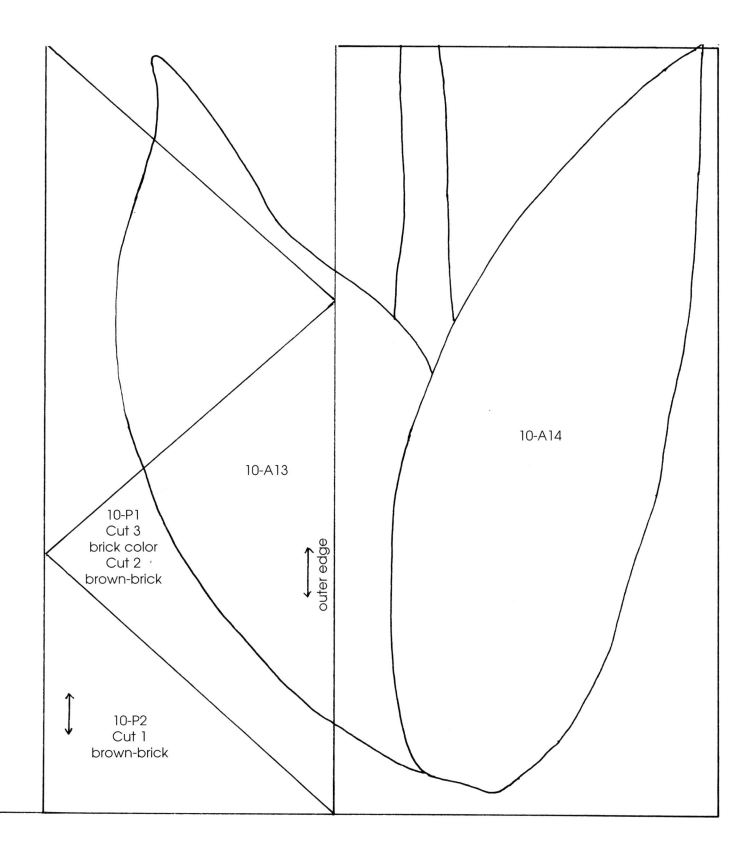

10-A14

10-A13

10-P1
Cut 3
brick color
Cut 2
brown-brick

10-P2
Cut 1
brown-brick

outer edge

Stemmed Flowers
Block 3

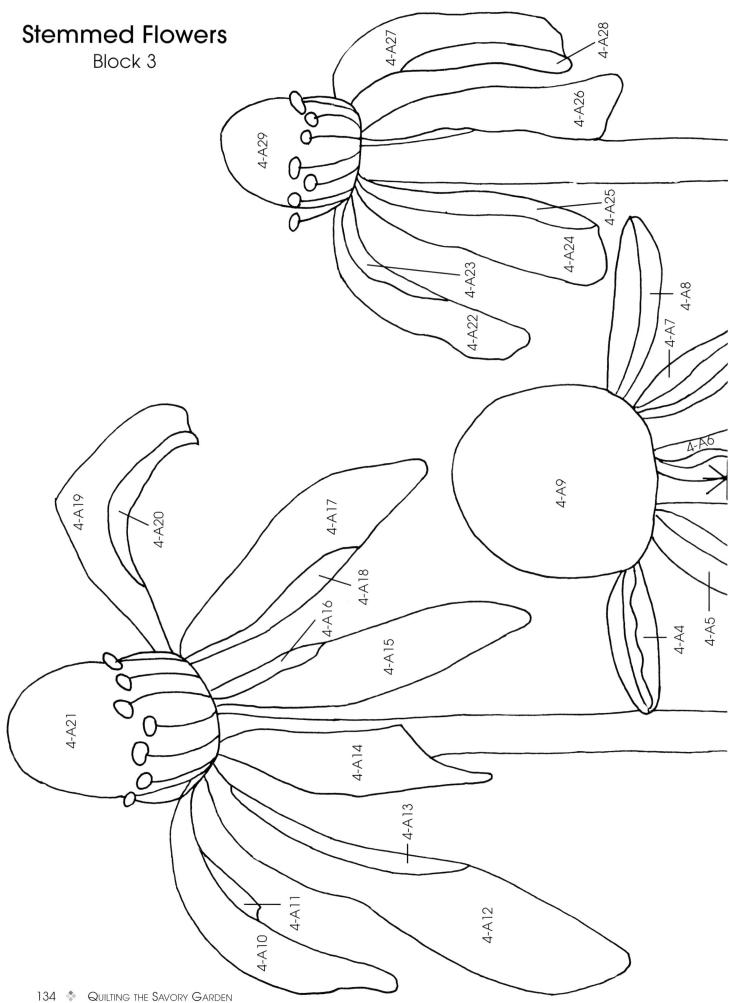

4-A27

4-A28

4-A26

4-A29

4-A25

4-A24

4-A23

4-A22

4-A8

4-A7

4-A19

4-A20

4-A17

4-A9

4-A18

4-A16

4-A15

4-A6

4-A21

4-A4

4-A5

4-A14

4-A13

4-A11

4-A10

4-A12

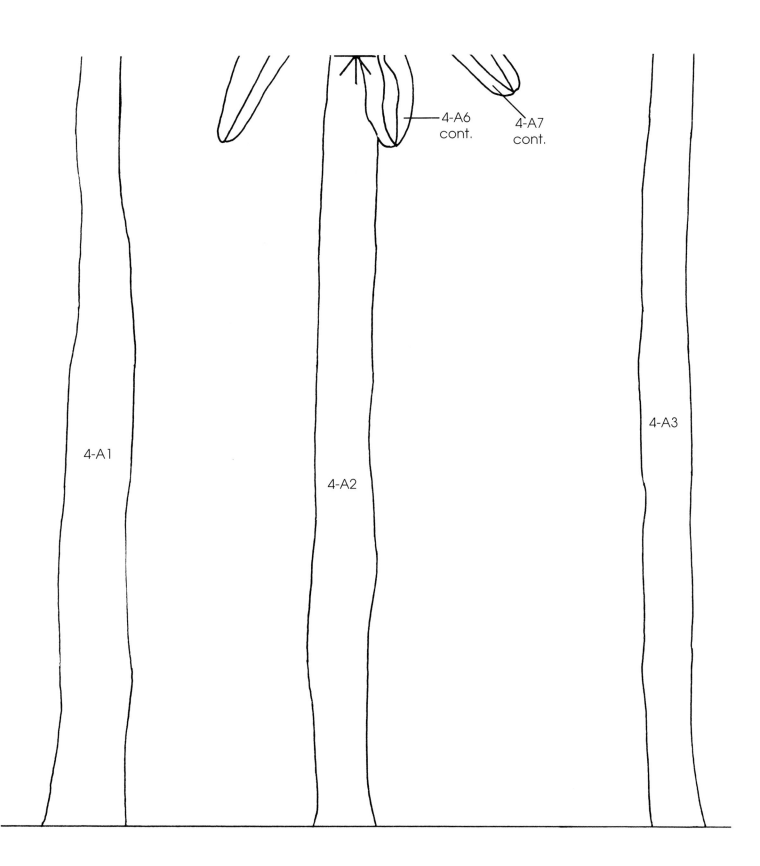

4-A6 cont.

4-A7 cont.

4-A3

4-A1

4-A2

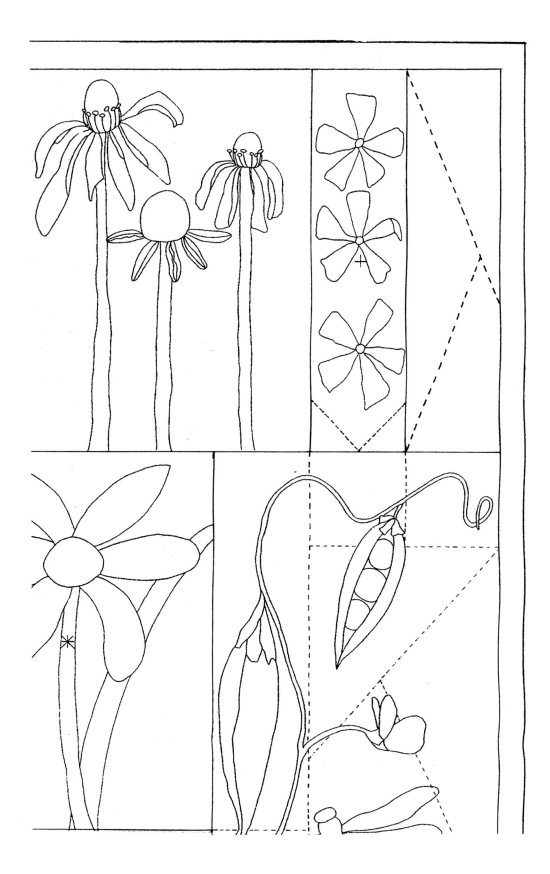

The Moss
Block 4

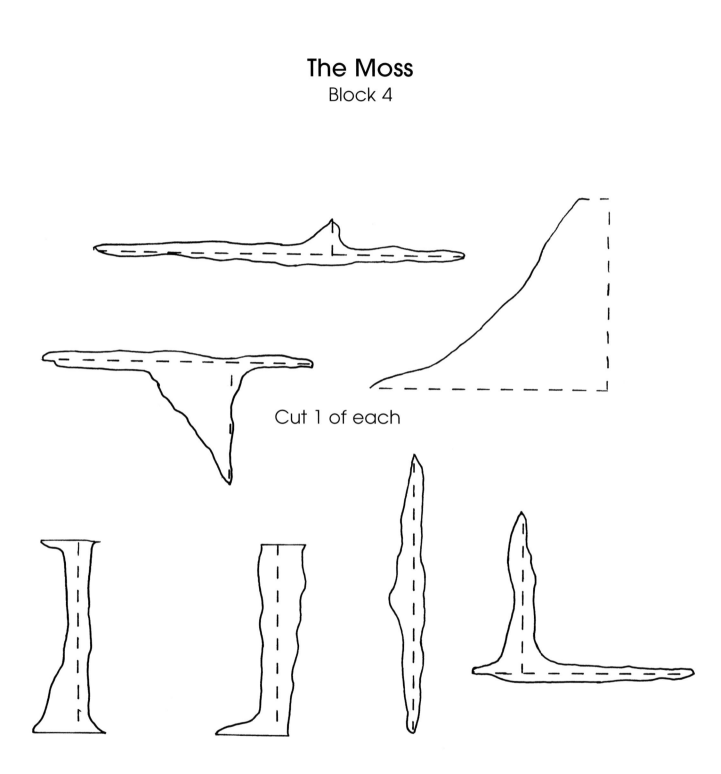

Cut 1 of each

Resources

Pfaff Sewing Machines
610 Winters Ave.
Paramus, NJ 07652
404-808-6550

Koala Cabinets (SCS USA)
9631 NE Colfax St.
Portland, OR 97220
800-547-8025

YLI Corporation
(Thread)
161 West Main St.
Rock Hill, SC 29730
803-985-3100

Clover Needlecraft, Inc.
1007 East Dominguez St., Ste. L
Carson, CA 90746-3620
310-516-7846

Creative Grids
(Rulers)
Checker Distributors
400-B W. Dussel Dr., Box 460
Maumee, OH 43537-0460
800-537-1060

Electric Quilt Company-EQ5
419 Gould St., Ste. 2
Bowling Green, OH 43402
www.electricquilt.com

Roxanne™ Products Company
(Glue-baste)
742 Granite Ave.
Lathrop, CA 95330
800-993-4445
www.thatperfectstitch.com

Index